W9-DAU-665

PUERTO RICO:
THE FOUR-STOREYED COUNTRY

PUERTO RICO

THE FOUR-STOREYED COUNTRY
and Other Essays

José Luis González

TRANSLATED BY GERALD GUINNESS

 Markus Wiener Publishing, Inc.
Princeton & New York

For information write to:
  Markus Wiener Publishing, Inc.
  114 Jefferson Road, Princeton, NJ 08540

Library of Congress Cataloging-in-Publication Data

González, José Luis, 1926–
      [Pais de cuatro pisos y otros ensayos. English]
      Puerto Rico: the four-storeyed country/José Luis González;
  translation and introduction by Gerald Guinness.
      Includes bibliographical references.
      ISBN 1-55876-072-5
      1. Puerto Rico—Civilization.   I. Title   II. Title: Four-storeyed
  country.
  F1960.G6613   1993
  972.95—dc20   92-45619
                                                          CIP

Printed in The United States of America

Contents

Introduction

Puerto Rico: The Four-Storeyed Country and Other Essays
is in no sense an introduction to the social or cultural history
of Puerto Rico; on the contrary it presupposes a good deal of
prior knowledge on the part of its readers. To read these
essays is to enter into the middle of a debate of long standing,
with much common ground taken for granted but with key
areas the subject of furious dispute. Perhaps the image we
need is of an ongoing family quarrel, where all the family
members have a common background and share certain
beliefs about what in the long run will benefit the family as
a whole, but where there are profound divergences between
the generations, or, as often happens, between even members
of the same generation, about how and for whose particular
advantage the benefit is to be distributed. For outside
observers it may seem at first glance that it is only these
divergences which really count, but this is to underestimate
the hidden bonds that hold this family to a common purpose.

In fact what the members of the family have in common is
the assumption that Puerto Rico is — or is on the way to
becoming — a nation, and that as a nation it has the right to
independence and to the free exercise of national
sovereignty. (Non-family members, who believe that Puerto
Rico should become a state of the U.S. or should continue as a
semi-autonomous dependency, aren't invited to join this
particular debate.) But beyond this unanimity as to the
desired end of national sovereignty, the *independentista*
family is wildly at odds on a variety of topics. For example,
it disagrees as to whether Uncle Aurelio was a hero or a
scoundrel, whether or not son Luis should be allowed to

marry a black girl, and what should be done about daughter
Dolores who persists on knowing people from "the wrong side
of the tracks" in the *caserío* or public housing project opposite
the family home. In other words, questions of history, race,
and class. To which, if we add questions of culture — for
example, father's *danzas* versus young Luis's *salsa* — we
have the ingredients for a furious family debate on what are
perhaps the most important issues of life, with the exception
of religion. (No wonder quarrels within this family often
strike outsiders as bitterer and more protracted than those
between the family as a whole and other families on the
same block!)

It is part of José Luis González's distinction that he has
given this debate a keener focus by foregrounding a topic
often neglected in a society skilled in the delicate art of
leaving certain things unsaid: the topic of *race*. González is
himself a man of mixed race, the son of a white Puerto Rican
father and a mestizo Dominican mother. The world he grew
up in was one where Puerto Rican "national culture," and so
by extension Puerto Rican national identity, was defined by
intellectuals in terms of the ideals and habits of a class that
was racially white. In the nineteenth century this class had
been predominantly a land-owning class, although this
century it has become increasingly urban and professional.
Finally, it was a class that, in its more literate reaches, had
resisted Spanish domination in the last century, but, by a
curious reversal, has become Hispanophile in this.
González's life and work may be read as an attempt to refute
such definitions and to replace them by definitions deriving
directly from the actual character and tastes of the great
majority of the Puerto Rican people, a majority that is black
and mestizo, that is proletarian, and that is contemptuous of
(or at the least indifferent to) a Spanish legacy that it
associates with the creole seignorial class from whose
hegemony it was delivered by the American invasion of

1898. For González, it is *this* constituency that should provide the basis for a national identity, and whose cultural habits should define a culture recognized as being of the nation as a whole.

González grounds his critique of the traditional *independentismo* definitions of national identity and national culture on an analysis of nineteenth-century demography. In the course of that century, he argues, two distinct racial and social groups could be distinguished: the black and mestizo peasantry, whom he calls the first Puerto Ricans because they were the first inhabitants who *had* to make the island their home (excluding of course the original Indian population who had been wiped out soon after the Spanish conquest), and a new class of white immigrants, encouraged to settle in Puerto Rico by the *Real Cédula de Gracias* of 1815, which was an attempt to "whiten" the population then thought to be tilting dangerously to the advantage of the blacks. (The Spanish authorities had witnessed the success of the recent black uprisings in Haiti and feared their repetition in Puerto Rico.) These are the "first" and "second" storeys of the Puerto Rican "house" referred to in the title essay. Two later storeys were subsequently superimposed: the first an urban professional class, and the second, in this century, a managerial class brought into being by Luis Muñoz Marín's economic policies of the 1940s on.

Essential to González's argument is the notion that many members of the "second storey," who before 1898 had been liberal and anti-Spanish, became after 1898 anti-American and conservative, a political transformation he ascribes to their progressive realization that they were doomed to marginalization by the economic and social policies of the new regime, which had as its results (among other things) the emancipation of the colored population and, in a more recent past, the emancipation of Puerto Rican women. Faced by this challenge to their hegemony the members of this endangered species evolved, with the help of their intellectuals, the comforting myth of a prelapsarian tellurist paradise now threatened by the divisive force of American capitalism. A telling example of this myth-making, quoted by González, is the reference made by the great nationalist leader of the 1930s, Pedro Albizu Campos, to "the old collective happiness" of the nineteenth century: in fact, González believes, it was Eugenio María de Hostos who was infinitely nearer the mark when he referred to the nineteenth century as a time when "life was lived under the sway of barbarity." For González this turnabout from nineteenth century realism to twentieth century myth-making constitutes a falsification of history and an insult to the memory of countless Puerto Ricans for whom life under the Spanish and white seignorial class, for the most part recent immigrants, had been anything but an "old collective happiness." What is now needed, he argues, is for such myths to be dismantled preparatory to a total restructuring of Puerto Rican society based on a *correct* interpretation of the national identity. For González this interpretation must pay homage to three salient facts: 1. that the national identity is primarily mestizo (i.e. of the "first storey"), with an enormously important, although insufficiently acknowledged, apportation from the black African element; 2. that national culture must be seen and defined as something rising "from below" rather than as something imposed by a white minority "from above"; and 3. that Puerto Ricans must acknowledge that their culture is primarily Caribbean rather than either North American (which for members of this particular family goes without saying) or Hispanic (which is still a matter of debate).

The second of these salient facts, that national culture should be defined as something rising "from below" rather than as something imposed "from above," might appear to need some clarificatory definition and it is here that

González's concept of "plebeyism," borrowed from the Spanish thinker José Ortega y Gasset, proves useful. Ortega had been struck by how in the late seventeenth and throughout the eighteenth centuries the Spanish popular classes, denied models of comportment and style by a decadent aristocracy no longer capable of setting an example, turned in upon themselves and "recreated for themselves a sort of second nature that was informed by qualities that were basically aesthetic." In other words, they created a culture that was more than merely a collection of distinctive habits but took on many of the attributes of what we sometimes call "high" culture: aesthetic grace, discipline, and formalized ritual. González sees the conditions that obtained in late seventeenth-century and eighteenth-century Spain as somewhat analogous to those obtaining in twentieth-century Puerto Rico. Because the Puerto Rican high bourgeoisie this century has no more been able to "set an example" that the Spanish aristocracy could in an earlier period, the popular classes have had to go it alone in the matter of creating cultural forms, evolving an autonomous cultural expression that González sees manifest in the Puerto Ricans' passion for sport, for music, and for the varying forms of show business or *farándula*. For him these are *plebeyist*, as opposed to *populist*, manifestations, since the latter term describes middle-class recreations of working-class mores whereas *plebeyist* refers to mores created by the popular classes for their own use, rising spontaneously from within their own ranks and, by a sort of sublimation, becoming in due course models for the society as a whole. Two specific examples of plebeyism González finds in the work of the painter José Rosa and the writer Luis Rafael Sánchez, author of the widely-read novel *La Guaracha del macho Camacho* (*Macho Camacho's Beat*). Here are artists who have created works of "high" culture by "assuming" (González's word) into their own persons the realities of which they treat, not necessarily to condone that reality (in Sánchez's case, very much the opposite) but so as to report on it from within rather than patronizing it *de haut en bas,* as in the past. Plebeyism, in short, is the first storey's reply to the casi-canonical claim, institutionalized in most literary histories, that the culture of the second and third storeys (the existence of a culture of the fourth storey being as yet moot) is *the* national culture. Not so! replies González, speaking on behalf of that first storey.

González's essays on the four storeys of Puerto Rican society and on plebeyism constitute his key contributions to the ongoing debate on how we may most aptly define the Puerto Rican national culture. A third essay, "Literature and National Identity," takes up these themes and gives them a particular application to a "national" literature. For González such a literature isn't what it is often claimed to be — a largely *costumbrista* or nativist literature, with the *jíbaro* or white peasant of the central mountain areas as its protagonist, and deriving ultimately from Manuel Alonso's *El gíbaro* published in 1843; it is, rather, a literature that takes its source in the work of Alejandro Tapia y Rivera (1826–82), which in its modernizing bias (particularly to be seen in its condemnation of slavery and relatively liberal attitude to women's rights), and in its correct naming of the evils of the nineteenth-century system, stays close to the realities of the national condition and truly foreshadows the desiderated multi-racial non-sexist society of the future. Once again González explains how this privileging, by the spokesmen of a presumed "national" culture, of the patently unrepresentative literary tradition of Alonso and *costum-brismo,* has been the result of what he calls an "ideological displacement" on the part of those spokesmen. A dominant caste, disappointed at its progressive marginalization after 1898, created a *jibarista* myth of social cohesion and rural felicity in defiance of the facts and to bolster up its own

position. More recently, however, by redefining Puerto Rican
national identity in terms of "the mulatto, conceived as the
defining synthesis of what is truly 'Puerto Rican,'" modern
writers (of whom González is of course one) have robbed the
jibarista myth of its validity and so have "closed the
parenthesis" of white cultural dominance first opened by the
promulgation of the *Real Cédula de Gracias* in 1815.

The remaining essays in *Puerto Rico: The Four-Storeyed
Country* add grace notes to this particular theme. In "The
'Lamento Borincano': A Sociological Interpretation"
González asks why this famous bolero by Puerto Rican
composer Rafael Hernández achieved such immense popularity throughout Latin America, expressing a protest on
behalf of, and appealing to, the common man, whereas the
nineteenth-century revolutionary poetry of Lola Rodríguez
and Pachín Marín has for the most part fallen on deaf ears.
This is once again proof, in González's opinion, that genuine
plebeyist art, which arises spontaneously from the people
and expresses the people's fears and aspirations with no itch
to preach or deliver a message, will always succeed,
whereas overtly propagandist art, however well inten-
tioned, can never capture the people's hearts. "On Puerto
Rican Literature of the 1950s" aligns the literature of his
own generation, the so-called "Generation of the '50s" (a
title he thoroughly dislikes, incidentally), with the
tradition of nineteenth-century fiction which told the truth
about the national condition: González argues that that
tradition, and its continuation in the work of the Generation
of the '50s stand in opposition to the myth-making literature
of a disappointed creole bourgeoisie to which we have
already referred.

In "Bernardo Vega: A Fighter and His People" González
carries the argument to New York City, penning a graceful
tribute to the posthumous memoirs of this veteran socialist
and profiting by the opportunity to explain how in New

York, too, there were alternative *independentismos*, that of the bourgeois conservatives, who were at once anti-American and racist, and that of the proletarian radicals, like Bernardo Vega himself. These latter individuals, pro-independence as they were, nonetheless saw themselves as "the historical product of the American regime" (an apparent anomaly González never tires of explaining) and New York, scene of their enforced emigration, as "their" town.

Finally, in "A Writer in Exile" González relates these themes to the facts of his own life and rounds on certain of his critics, who complain about his prolonged residence in Mexico and at the fact that two of his recent stories do not deal with "Puerto Rican subjects." For González, such "primitive nationalism" is one more symptom of the basic conservatism that characterizes the creole bourgeois independence movement, with its idealization of a non-existent past and its inability either to understand or to identify with the aspirations of the masses. Failing to understand the national condition, this independence movement has found itself unable to "unleash a truly effective anticolonial struggle" and is hence doomed to political and ideological irrelevance in the years to come. "What such a situation naturally requires is the re-examination of the national condition from the foundations up," is how the book ends — a phrase that may be taken as the motto for González's work as a whole, devoted as it has been to re-examining the national condition "from the foundations up."

The publication of *Purto Rico: The Four-Storeyed Country* in 1980 under its original title, *El país de cuatro pisos* set off a frenzied debate on the subject of the "four storeys" of the Puerto Rican mansion, a debate which has not quite exhausted itself even after the passage of a decade. Criticism of González's thesis has taken several forms. Some of it, from the "opposition" camp — i.e. from anti-independentists — has been entirely predictable and needn't perhaps be summarized in this Introduction, which has taken as its starting point the assumption that this was a debate between members of the same "family" or, in other words, those who shared the same broad objectives with respect to nationhood and national independence. There were, however, certain objections to the book from *within* the family that must be noted, however briefly.

One recurring criticism of *Puerto Rico: The Four-Storeyed Country* concerns González's treatment of Pedro Albizu Campos. Why (this objection runs) should Albizu, the most fervent and effective advocate of Puerto Rican independence this century, be severed from the noble independentist tradition of Betances and Hostos and relegated to a limbo of political "conservatism"? Remember Albizu took on the American Goliath in face-to-face and highly unequal combat: is it reasonable to demand that in addition to this resistance, and to his noble defense of Spanish at the time when it was most in danger, Albizu should also have had up-to-the-minute views on the class struggle? And (the criticism concludes) hard as González is on Albizu, he is considerably less hard on the Communist Party of his own day, which itself had a great deal to answer for. In the experience of the present writer, it is very often the issue of whether or not González has been fair to Albizu Campos that arises in question time whenever the author of *Puerto Rico: The Four-Storeyed Country* goes on the lecture circuit to defend his views.

Perhaps a more damaging critique concerns the methodology González adopts in *Puerto Rico: The Four-Storeyed Country*. González has been condemned for postulating a rough division between a black and mulatto "first storey" and a white "second storey," which he largely abandons as he gets nearer the present day. (In general, it is claimed, his evocation of the third and fourth

since 1898 is very much more cursory than his earlier
evocation of the first and second storeys on which they rest.)
For some critics this "two nation" thesis, which postulates a
white creole minority sitting on the backs of a black mestizo
majority, has been unduly influenced by similar two-nation
theories employed in South and Central America, where the
large Indian popu-lations obviously give the model a high
degree of validity. Nor, say the same critics, does González's
distinction between "a culture of the élite" and "a culture of
the masses" have anything like the rigor that the more
traditional Marxist categories of socio-economic classes bring
to the analysis of the social composition of a society. This,
they claim, is particularly misleading the nearer González
approaches the present day, where an élite/masses dichot-
omy simply won't explain the infinite complexity of a
society that changes its composition, its contours, and its
cultural preferences, by the hour. For these critics, a more
traditional analysis in terms of *class* would have thrown
more light on what is happening in the Puerto Rico of today
than González's somewhat confusing analysis conducted in
terms of *culture.*

A related difficulty has been González's theme of a
"plebeyist" culture, borrowed from Ortega to describe
conditions basically different from those Ortega originally
envisaged. For example, to take a writer as refined and
cultured as Luis Rafael Sánchez as the epitome of a new
spirit of "plebeyism" in Puerto Rican literature poses certain
problems, as does too the concept of how writers and artists
"assume" proletarian qualities into their work by a sort of
osmosis. Then again, González's negative attempt to
discredit the creole bourgeoisie's claim that the culture of
their class is *the* national culture has struck some critics as
more persuasive than his positive attempt to evoke a
national culture of the people that wells up from the lower
depths like water from a hidden spring. (And, they say,

González doesn't always concede how *dirty* that water often is, with this "plebeyist" culture constantly sullied by cultural garbage flowing into it from the mainland.) Finally, González's parting shot on the last page of his book that on the national issue certain of his contemporaries never manage to see the wood for the trees has bred resentment among independentists who argue that living among the trees (i.e. at home in Puerto Rico rather than in exile) is perhaps the best way there is for getting a good sense of the changing shape and composition of the wood as a whole.*

Readers of *Puerto Rico: The Four-Storeyed Country* will have to make up their minds on these as on other issues raised by the book and if they are impartial observers they may well decide (perhaps the path of wisdom for anyone who gets involved in a family debate) that González gets it right in certain respects, but gets it wrong in others. What isn't however in doubt is the immense stimulus the book, taken in conjunction with *Conversación con José Luis González* by Arcadio Díaz Quiñones (1976) and *Nueva visita al cuarto piso* (1986) by González himself, has given to thinking about the issues of the national identity and the national culture. The important thing is that José Luis González has initiated a debate — or to put it more exactly, has given new life and a sparkling new focus to a debate that had threatened to become repetitive and sterile. For that, members of the Puerto Rican independentist family and even those outsiders who have strayed in from the street are all greatly in his debt.

— Gerald Guinness

---

*For these criticisms, see in particular the final chapter of José Luis Méndez's *Para una sociologia de la literatura puertorriqueña*, Cuadernos Casa, 1982 and his unpublished paper, "Sobre pisos y prosas: reflexiones en torno al libro 'Nueva visita al cuarto piso' de José Luis González."

Puerto Rico: The Four-Storeyed Country

(Notes Toward a Definition of Puerto Rican Culture)

... history was political propaganda, it was used to create the national unity, in other words the nation itself, from without and in despite of tradition, laying its foundations on literature and saying "I *want* things to be this way," not "This is the way they *should* be, given existing conditions." The intellectuals, because they shared this position, had to distance themselves from the masses, stand aside, create or strengthen among themselves the spirit of caste, so that they came to *distrust* the masses, feel them as alien, be fearful of them — because for the intellectuals the masses were an unknown quantity, a mysterious hydra of innumerable heads.... By contrast ... many intellectual movements aimed at modernizing and at de-rhetoricizing culture and bringing it closer to the masses, nationalizing it, one might say. ("Nation-masses" and "nation-rhetoric" might serve as approximate labels for these two tendencies.)

Antonio Gramsci, *Letters from Prison* (III,82)

In September 1979 I was conducting a seminar in Latin-American Studies at the University of Puerto Rico. A group of Puerto Rican students in this seminar, enrolled in the social science faculty of the university but mostly graduates of various schools at the National Autonomous University of Mexico, put the following question to me in the course of our discussions: *How, as you see it, has American colonial intervention affected Puerto Rican culture and what do you*

1

think about the present state of that culture? The essay that follows is my attempt to provide an answer to this question. I have sub-titled it "Notes Toward a Definition of Puerto Rican Culture" because all I aim to do in this essay is suggest the nucleus for an interpretive study of the historical and cultural realities of Puerto Rico, something that I am sure requires a more sustained analysis and more carefully reasoned conclusions than anything I can provide here. Still, I hope that this essay, in spite of its limited scope, may prove useful for the members of the Latin-American Studies seminar and for any other readers who may decide to honor it with their critical attention.

* * *

As we all know, the question you students asked me raises an enormously important issue that has preoccupied and continues to preoccupy those many Puerto Ricans who are involved, from a variety of ideological standpoints, in the Puerto Rican situation and who are naturally concerned with how that situation will develop. But before attempting an answer I asked myself (as I am sure you asked yourselves before passing the question on to me) what you really meant by the phrase "Puerto Rican culture." It struck me that you might not mean exactly what I mean by it and so I thought it wise to tackle that difficulty first since I suspect that everything I shall go on to say is the rough sketch of a thesis in direct contradiction to what most Puerto Rican intellectuals have for many decades taken to represent established truths, and even, sometimes, articles of patriotic faith. I shall therefore try to be as explicit as possible within the brief space that a reply of this nature allows — which, let me again stress, makes no claim to being definitive but aims only at providing a starting-point for a dialogue that I feel sure will remain cordial in spite of any valid and productive differences of opinion between us.

Let me begin, then, by agreeing wholeheartedly with the idea, held by many sociologists, that there co-exist two separate cultures at the heart of any society divided into classes, a culture of the oppressors and another culture of the oppressed. Now it is clear that these two cultures, precisely because they *co*-exist, aren't to be seen as watertight compartments; in fact they are more like intercommunicating vessels between which there is a constant reciprocal flow. The dialectical nature of that flow usually gives the impression of homogeneity, but in fact no such homogeneity really exists — indeed it could only exist in a society *without* classes, and only then after a long process of consolidation. By contrast, in any society *with* classes the true relation between the two cultures in that society is one of dominance, with the culture of the oppressors dominating and the culture of the oppressed being dominated. It follows that what is often passed off as "the general culture," even as "the national culture," is, naturally enough, merely a description of but one of these cultures — the dominant culture of the oppressors. So I really cannot begin to answer the question you put to me without first trying to determine precisely what that "national culture" was really like at the time of the American arrival in Puerto Rico, although here too, if we are to treat this issue with the seriousness it merits, we first have to make sure we know the answer to another question: Just what sort of a "nation" *was* Puerto Rico in 1898?

Needless to say, many Puerto Ricans have asked that question before and their answers to it have been various and sometimes contradictory. (I am speaking, of course, of those Puerto Ricans who have conceived of Puerto Rico as a nation; those who have denied the existence of such a nation, last century and this, pose a problem that should also be analyzed, although for the moment I intend to leave it to one side.) To make a start, then, let us consider two important figures who both *did* conceive of Puerto Rico as a nation: Eugenio María de Hostos and Pedro Albizu Campos.

For Hostos in 1898, what the Spanish colonial regime had left in Puerto Rico was a society "where life was lived under the sway of barbarity"; barely three decades later Albizu Campos defined the social reality of that same regime as "the old collective happiness." How is one to explain the extreme contradiction between such statements by two honorable and intelligent men, both of whom struggled to achieve the same political goal, the independence of Puerto Rico? If we recognize, as I believe we must, that it was Hostos who stuck close to the historical truth and Albizu who distorted it, and if we don't wish to fall into subjective interpretations which apart from possibly turning out to be wrong would be unjust, then we should look for explanations of this contradiction in the historical processes that caused it rather than in the personalities who gave it expression. In other words, it is not so much a matter of Hostos versus Albizu as of one historical vision versus another historical vision.

Let us begin by asking ourselves about the state of affairs that prompted Hostos to stick to the historical truth in his opinion about the condition of Puerto Rico at the time of the American invasion. In other words, what permitted Hostos to recognize, without thereby betraying his belief in Puerto Rican independence, that in 1898 "the social and individual weakness one sees on every hand seems to render our people incapable of helping themselves?" What permitted such critical frankness was without a doubt his vision of the stage Puerto Rico had then reached in the course of its political evolution. It was the vision of a society only just beginning its journey toward nationhood and then wracked by enormous collective ills (the ills Manuel Zeno Gandía denounced in his novels dealing with "a sick world" and that Salvador Brau analyzed in his "sociological disquisitions"). If the nineteenth-century Puerto Rican separatists with Ramón Emeterio Betances at their head believed in and fought for national independence, it was because they understood that independence was necessary to carry forward to completion the forging of a national identity, not because any of them believed that such a national identity already existed. Not confusing politics with sociology, the separatists knew that with Puerto Rico, as with Latin-America as a whole, the creation of a national State was intended not so much to express an already fully-formed national identity as to provide the most potent and effective means of stimulating and completing the creation of that identity. In fact, *no* Latin-American country that century had arrived at independence as the culmination of a process of creating a national identity, but only by previously having forged political and judicial institutions to foster and encourage that same process.

Be that as it may, the fact remains that the Puerto Rican separatists never achieved any such independence and still today many supporters of Puerto Rican independence wonder why. Some continue to think it was because somebody or other betrayed the rebellion at Lares, or that the five hundred rifles that Betances had loaded on a boat in Saint Thomas didn't reach Puerto Rico in time. Others think it was because twenty years afterwards Puerto Rican separatists were fighting in Cuba rather than in their own country, or . . . who knows how many other "reasons," all equally foreign to any truly scientific conception of history? But in fact the only *real* reason the separatists never achieved independence in the nineteenth century is the reason that was offered on more than one occasion by that revolutionary hero who, after his first defeat, acquired the wise habit of never pulling the wool over his own eyes: Ramón Emeterio

Betances himself. The reason (and this is a direct quotation from this father of the separatist cause) is that "Puerto Ricans don't want [their] independence." But what do such words mean when spoken or written by a man like Betances, a man who insisted that independence was the only just and reasonable destiny for his country and who viewed that independence as Puerto Rico's necessary first step toward her incorporation into the great Antillean federation? Who exactly were those "Puerto Ricans" Betances was talking about — and what did he mean by saying they "don't want [their] independence?"

Betances himself explained what he meant soon after the uprising at Lares in a letter from Port-au-Prince in which he attributed the failure of this uprising to the fact that "the rich Puerto Ricans have abandoned us." Betances didn't have to be a Marxist to know that in his day and age a revolution against the colonial powers was doomed to failure without the support of the creole ruling class. In Puerto Rico it was precisely the members of *this* class who "didn't want [their] independence." They didn't want it because they *couldn't* want it, because their weakness as a class, determined fundamentally though not exclusively by Puerto Rico's weak economic substructure, didn't allow the ruling class to go beyond the reformist yearnings which had always characterized it. The relative development of the economy between 1868 and 1887 and consequently of the ideology of the landowning and professional class — what then most closely resembled an incipient national bourgeoisie — is what determined the shift from assimilationism to autonomism in the political attitudes of that class. But these landowners and professionals never went as far as to believe, not even by 1898, that Puerto Rico had become a nation capable, as an independent State, of guiding its own destinies. In the case of Hostos, then, the desire for independence was never at odds with a realistic appraisal of the historical situation he lived through. And it was this appraisal that led Hostos to declare in 1898, when after an exile of several decades he came face-to-face with Puerto Rican reality, that the Puerto Rican people were incapable of governing themselves and so to propose, to overcome this incapacity, a program of moral and physical regeneration which he believed could be completed in twenty years, if the time were well employed.

By contrast, the time Albizu had to live through some thirty years later was characterized not only by the political immaturity of the creole ruling class (whose members Albizu had hoped to mobilize in the struggle for independence) but by an even more disheartening feature — the co-option, disenfranchisement, and subsequent crippling of that class by the irruption of imperialist American capitalism into Puerto Rico. Angel Quintero Rivera has admirably explained the political and economic aspects of this process by showing clearly how the ever-growing economic weakness of the creole ruling class rendered it incapable of countering American imperialism with a plan of its own for the historical development of Puerto Rico and in fact finally led it to abandon the liberalism that characterized it in the last century, for the conservatism that has so far characterized it in this. The idealization — or rather, the misrepresentation — of the historical past has always been one of the typical traits of the ideology of this ruling class. Pedro Albizu Campos was without a doubt the most coherent and consistent spokesman for that conservative ideology — conservative in content, that is, but in Albizu's case radical in expression, since he spoke on especial behalf of the most desperate members of that class (and I owe that very precise adjective "desperate" to the distinguished nationalist poet Juan Antonio Corretjer). That historical desperation, so understandable that there is no reason why it should come as a surprise to anyone, was what forced Albizu to distort the truth by calling the Spanish colonial regime in Puerto Rico "the old collective happiness."

Now we can turn to the relevance all this has to the problem of the Puerto Rican "national culture" today. If Puerto Rican society has always been a society divided into classes, and if, as we maintained earlier, there are in every class-divided society two cultures, the culture of the oppressors and the culture of the oppressed, moreover if what is known as "national culture" is generally the oppressing culture — then it is necessary to recognize that what in Puerto Rico we have always called "the national culture" is in fact nothing more than the culture of that class of landowners and professional men to which I have already referred. One should, however, make one thing clear about our use of the term "oppressors" and "oppressed" in the Puerto Rican context, which is that there is no denying the fact that the creole oppressors at home have at the same time been subject to oppression from abroad. It is precisely this that explains the cultural achievements of this class last century. These achievements, insofar as they expressed a resistance to Spanish domination, were essentially progressive, given the totally reactionary nature in all respects of that domination. But the same class that was oppressed by the imperial power was in turn oppressing one other social class in Puerto Rico, the class made up of slaves, until their emancipation in 1873, of landless laborers, and of small craftsmen. (As for industrial workers, strictly speaking, there were very few of them in nineteenth-century Puerto Rico, given the country's almost total lack of what could be called modern industries.) The "culture of the oppressed" in Puerto Rico has been and is the culture produced by this "other social class" I have just mentioned. (As a matter of fact, it is a culture that has been studied by the ruling class intellectuals only as *folklore*, that invention of the European bourgeoisie which has served so well to spirit away the true significance of popular culture.) And from now on, so as to avoid misunderstandings, let us refer to these two cultures, of oppressors and oppressed, as respectively "élite culture" and "popular culture."

To answer your question we must first examine, even if it has to be in a somewhat schematic form due to lack of space, how each of these two cultures came into being and how it subsequently developed. The obvious thing would be to start with the popular culture, for the simple reason that of the two it was born first. It is by now a commonplace to assert that this culture has three historical roots: the Taino Indian, the African, and the Spanish. What isn't however a commonplace — in fact just the opposite — is to say that of these three roots the one that is most important, for economic and social — and hence cultural — reasons, is the African. As is well known, the indigenous population of Puerto Rico was wiped out in a matter of mere decades by the genocidal brutality of the Spanish Conquest. (Well known *as a piece of information,* though without a doubt poorly assimilated both morally and intellectually, to judge by the fact that the principal avenue of our capital city still bears the name of that greedy adventurer and enslaver of Indians, Juan Ponce de León.)

The extermination of the Indian population couldn't of course keep aboriginal elements from figuring in our definition as a people, but it seems clear to me that their contribution to our Puerto Rican identity was achieved primarily by cultural exchange between the Indians and the other two ethnic groups, in particular the blacks, because Indians and blacks had been trapped in the most oppressed stratum of the social pyramid during the early period of colonization and therefore had more contact with one another than either had with the dominant Spanish group. It is also well known, because it has been documented, that the composition of the Spanish group was exceptionally unstable throughout the first two centuries of colonial life. For example, it is worth remembering that in 1534 the governor of the colony gave an account of his efforts to stop the Spanish population's mass exodus to the mainland in search of riches. The island, he wrote, was "so depopulated that one sees hardly any people of Spanish descent, but only Negroes." The Spanish ingredient, then, in the formation of a popular Puerto Rican culture must have taken the form of agricultural laborers, mostly from the Canary Islands, imported to the island when the descendants of the first African slaves *had already become black Puerto Ricans*. It is because of this that I believe, as I have said on various occasions to the embarrassment and irritation of some, that the first Puerto Ricans were in fact *black* Puerto Ricans. I am not claiming, needless to say, that these first Puerto Ricans had any idea of a "national homeland," for in fact *no one* at that time in Puerto Rico entertained, or could have entertained, such an idea. What I *am* claiming is that it was the blacks, the people bound most closely to the territory which they inhabited (they were after all slaves), who had the greatest difficulty in imagining any other place to live. Of course, it might be argued against this line of reasoning that the goal of several of the slave conspiracies that took place in Puerto Rico in the nineteenth century — at least according to the statements of official documents — was to escape to Santo Domingo, where slavery had been abolished. But it shouldn't be forgotten that many of these conspiracies were led either by slaves born in Africa, the so-called *bozales,* or by slaves imported from other Caribbean islands, *not* by *negros criollos* or creole blacks, the name given to blacks born on the island before it became customary to recognize them as *Puerto Ricans.*

As for the white *campesinos* or countrymen of those early times, in other word the first "*jíbaros,*" the truth is that this was a poor peasantry that found itself obliged to adopt many of the life-habits of those other poor people already living in the country, namely the slaves. In this connection, it is not irrelevant to point out that when people today speak for example of "*jíbaro* food," what they really mean is "black food": plantains, rice, codfish, *funche,* etc. If the "national cuisine" of all the Caribbean islands and the bordering mainland territories is virtually the same in using certain basic ingredients albeit with slight though often imaginative variants, even though the territories were colonized by European nations of such widely differing culinary traditions as the Spanish, French, English and Dutch, then I think this can be explained by the fact that all we Caribbeans eat and drink today more like blacks than like Europeans. The same thing, or something quite similar, can be said of the Puerto Rican "national dress," the characteristics of which, to my knowledge, the folklorists haven't yet accurately defined. The truth is that the white *campesinos* for strictly economic reasons had to wear the same simple, comfortable, cheap clothing that the blacks wore. The upper-class creole tended to dress as a European as soon as that was feasible, and, as any Puerto Rican of my own generation with a good memory can confirm, the popular *guayabera* or embroidered shirt of our own day arrived on the island only three decades ago from Cuba, where it had been created as a garment for casual use among country landowners.

Throughout the first three centuries of our post-Columbian history Puerto Rican popular culture, which was essentially Afro-Antillean in character, defined us as just another Caribbean population. And the social majority which produced that culture also produced the first great historical figure in Puerto Rico, Miguel Henríquez, a mulatto shoemaker who became the richest man on the island during the second half of the eighteenth century thanks to his extraordinary energies as smuggler and pirate. (Richest, that is, until the Spanish authorities became alarmed at his power and decided to remove him, first from the island and then from this world.) Our first important artist also came from this same class: José Campeche, the mulatto son of an *esclavo "coartado"* or "limited slave," i.e. a slave purchasing his liberty in installments. And if after that Puerto Rican society had gone on evolving in the same way other Caribbean islands did, then our current "national culture" would be like theirs, a popular mestizo culture of a predominantly Afro-Antillean type.

But Puerto Rican society didn't in fact evolve this way in the course of the eighteenth and nineteenth centuries. At the beginning of the nineteenth century, when no one in Puerto Rico was thinking about a "national culture," what one might call a *second storey* — in social, economic, cultural, and as a result of all these factors, ultimately political, terms — was being added on to our national culture. A wave of immigrants fleeing from Spanish colonies then fighting for independence in South America began building and furnishing this second storey, joined almost immediately afterward, under the aegis of the *Real Cédula de Gracias* of 1815, by numerous foreigners (English, French, Dutch, Irish, etc.) and with a second wave, composed mainly of Corsicans, Majorcans, and Catalans, following them about the middle of the century.

This second wave of immigrants created virtually a second colonization, this time in the mountainous central area of the island. The institution of the *libreta* or pass-book contributed to this colonization by creating a workforce at once stable, and, needless to say, servile. The world of the coffee plantations, in this century mythicized as the epitome of "Puerto Ricanness," was in reality a world dominated by foreigners, whose wealth was founded on the expropriation of the old creole landlords and on the ruthless exploitation of a native campesino-class then existing on a subsistence level. (A splendid portrayal of this world is to be found in Fernando Picó's recent book *Libertad y servidumbre en el Puerto Rico del siglo XIX*, Ediciones Huracán, Río Piedras, 1979).

These new Spanish, Corsican, and Majorcan coffee-plantation owners were inevitably among the main props of the Spanish colonial regime and the culture they produced was, for equally natural reasons, a seignorial culture that looked abroad for its cultural norms. Even at the end of the century the Majorcan coffee growers spoke Majorcan among themselves and only used Spanish when they wanted to be understood by their Puerto Rican workers. And until well into the twentieth century, as many literary and historical sources attest, the Corsicans were perceived as foreigners, often as "Frenchmen," by the native Puerto Ricans. As for the Majorcans, it's enough to point to a historical fact which merits a good deal of socio-historical examination: many of these emigrants were what in Majorca are known as *chuetas*, i.e. the descendants of converted Jews. What I am getting at is this: What social attitudes would result when a minority discriminated against in its country of origin became, as the result of emigration, a *privileged* minority in its new home? We could, of course, ask the same question about the Corsican immigrants, who were either semi- or wholly-illiterate peasants in their native country and who became gentleman landowners after a few years in Puerto Rico. The poverty of the culture which this landlord class on the coffee plantations produced throughout the second half of the nineteenth century, when compared to the culture produced by the social élite in the coastal areas, reveals a class, in social and human terms, that was basically uncultured, arrogant, and conservative, and that despised and oppressed the native poor, and were, in turn, hated by them. It is this hatred, among other things, that explains the "seditious bands" that in 1898 attacked coffee plantations in the mountainous "uplands" of the island.

I have just mentioned 1898 — and this brings us, after our necessary historical excursion, to the gist of the question you asked me earlier. I began to answer by saying that in order to describe Puerto Rico's "national culture" at the time of the American invasion, it would first be necessary to ask what kind of a nation Puerto Rico was at that time. Well then, in the light of everything I have just said it seems no exaggeration to state that Puerto Rico was a country so divided racially, socially, economically, and culturally, that it should rather be described as *two* countries than as one. Or more precisely, perhaps, as two distinct societies that hadn't yet had time to fuse into a true national synthesis. But then this shouldn't surprise anyone, since such a phenomenon is not at all exclusive to Puerto Rico but is typical of Latin America as a whole. Mexico and Peru, for example, are still debating the problem of the "different countries": that of the Indians, that of the creoles, and that of the mestizos. In Argentina there is a long-standing conflict between the "old creoles" and the more recent immigrants and their descendants. In Haiti there is a notorious rivalry between blacks and mulattos. And so on.

What sets the Puerto Rican case apart is that for more than half a century we have been peddled the myth of social, racial, and cultural homogeneity which it is now high time that we began to dismantle, not so as to "divide" the country — a prospect that some people contemplate with terror — but rather so as to gain a true perspective on the country's real and objective diversity. Were we to imagine two contrasting Puerto Rican types as for example a (white) poet from Lares and a (black or mulatto) stevedore from Puerta de Tierra, we would immediately have to admit that there is a great difference between them, and I submit that it is a difference of a historically-determined *cultural tradition*, which must in no way be underestimated. (None of this implies, let me state bluntly to avoid any misunderstanding, that the one is necessarily "more Puerto Rican" than the other.) The difference I have referred to ultimately derives from two visions of the world, two *Weltanschauungen*, that are diametrically opposed in many important respects. All thinking Puerto Ricans, and more especially independentists, are distressed, and rightly so, by our people's persistent inability to agree on the final political organization of the country — in other words, the so-called "issue of status." In this sense at least we are responding to the reality of a "divided people." But what we haven't yet been able to recognize are the profound causes, the profound *historical* causes, of that division.

The traditional independence movement has maintained that this division only came into being because of the American invasion, and that what characterized Puerto Rican society during the Spanish colonial period was, in the words of Albizu Campos, "a homogeneity among all the components and a highly developed social sense dedicated to mutual aid for the perpetuation and preservation of our nation, in other words a deeply-rooted and unanimous sense of fatherland." Only the obfuscating power of a profoundly conservative ideology could have produced a view of things so essentially at variance with historical reality. All mythologizing apart, the Puerto Rico of 1898 can only, in fact, be described as a country *on the way to nationhood*. So Hostos saw it and Hostos was right. And if during the nineteenth century this process of nation-building suffered profound setbacks because of the two great waves of immigrants who, to repeat my metaphor, built a second storey on Puerto Rican society, then what happened in 1898 was that the American invasion began to add a *third* storey to a second which was still not entirely habitable.

To repeat: in this nation-in-the-making, divided as we know, or should know, not only into classes but also into distinct ethnic groups which were true castes, the two cultures of which I speak always coexisted. But precisely because we are dealing with a nation-in-the-making, these two cultures were not in themselves homogeneous. To start with, the social élite was divided into two clearly distinguishable groups: plantation-owners and professional men. Quintero Rivera has explained with great clarity how these two groups of the élite were ideologically distinct, with the landowners inclining more to conservatism and the professionals to liberalism. And when we come to culture, what must be stressed is that the culture of the landowners was above all a *way of life*, seignorial and conservative. The landowners themselves weren't capable of creating a literature that would describe or extol that way of life, and so this task fell, well into the present century, upon their descendants, members of a class in decline (but in decline *as a class* let it be understood, because individually the grandchildren of the "ruined" landowners, now become for the most part professionals, managers, or bureaucrats, enjoyed a standard of living much higher than any known to their grandparents). Only by seeing things in such a light can one understand, for example, the ideological content of a literary work such as René Marqués's *Los soles truncos.*

By contrast, the culture produced by the nineteenth-century professional men consisted of *creative works* and of *institutions*: virtually all our literature of this period, the Atheneum, and so on. And in these creative works and institutions it was the liberal ideology of their creators that predominated, with the result that "the culture of the dominant class" in nineteenth-century Puerto Rican colonial society isn't necessarily synonymous with "a reactionary culture." (It is very important to get this last point clear so as to avoid the simplifications and confusions peculiar to a certain type of underdeveloped "Marxism.") There certainly *were* reactionaries among cultivated Puerto Ricans at this time, but they neither formed a majority nor were they typical. Those who *did* form a majority and those who *were* typical were both liberal and progressive: Alonso, Tapia, Hostos, Brau, Zeno. . . .

Then, too, there were of course some revolutionaries, but these were in the minority and, characteristically and revealingly, often mestizos: one has only to think of Betances, of Pachín Marín, and of an artisan like Sotero Figueroa who mixed culturally with the élite. The most radical of the autonomists — and who will dare say it was by chance? — were also mestizos; just recall Baldorioty and Barbosa, whom conservative independentists have so misunderstood and slighted this century, the former as a "reformer" and the latter as a "Yankophile." (As though at least half of the separatists in the nineteenth century hadn't wanted to break with Spain so as to become part of the United States, in those days a shining symbol of republican democracy for most of the enlightened world!) There is the revealing history, for those who don't insist on ignoring the truth, of the Puerto Rican section of the Cuban Revolutionary Party in New York, where until 1898 separatist-independentists like Sotero Figueroa made common cause with separatist-annexionists (perhaps a grammatical but not a political contradiction) like Todd and Henna. (And don't these very names clearly speak to us of that "second storey" added by immigrants to Puerto Rican society in the early and middle years of the century?)

All this might seem, but in fact isn't, a digression, for Puerto Rican "national culture" at about the time of the 1898 invasion consisted of all these elements. That is to say, in its strengths, weaknesses and contradictions it was an exact reflection of that social class which gave it life. And if that class, as we have argued, can be characterized by its historical weakness and immaturity, could the culture that resulted possibly have been strong and mature? What gave

the culture a *relative* strength and maturity was, first, the
fact that it had its roots in an old, rich European culture,
namely the Spanish; and second, that it had already begun
to put its own creole stamp, in an Hispano-Antillean sense, on
whatever it produced. This last fact is undeniable and for
that reason those who maintain, or at any rate maintained
two or three decades ago, that there is no such thing as a
"national culture" in Puerto Rico are obviously wrong. But
wrong, too, are those who ignored and continue to ignore the
class basis of such a culture and describe it as the *only* culture
of the Puerto Rican people, identifying its decline under the
American colonial regime with a presumed decline in
national identity. Seeing things in this way not only confuses
the part with the whole, because that culture has in fact
only been *part* of what in an all-inclusive sense might be
called the "Puerto Rican national culture" — it certainly
can't claim to represent *all* the island's culture — but it also
fails to recognize the existence of the *other* Puerto Rican culture which under the American colonial regime has under-
gone not so much a deterioration as a development, an uneven
development no doubt and one that has been full of vicissitudes but a development none the less. And to say this is not,
as certain conservative patriots insist, to make a leftist
apol-ogy for American colonialism, but merely to recognize a
historical fact: the progressive dismantling of the culture of
the Puerto Rican élite under the impact of the transformations in Puerto Rican society resulting from the American
colonial presence has resulted less in the "Americanization"
of Puerto Rican society than in a transformation of cultural
values *from within.* The vacuum created by the dismantling
of the culture of the Puerto Rican élite hasn't been filled (far
from it) by intrusions of American culture; on the contrary,
what *has* filled that vacuum has been the ever more
perceptible rise to prominence of the culture of the Puerto
Rican lower classes.

We must now ask how and why such a thing came about. I see no way of giving a valid answer to this question except by putting it in the context of the class struggle which lies at the heart of Puerto Rican society. It is high time we began to understand, in the light of a scientific theory of history, just what the change of colonial regime in 1898 really meant for Puerto Rico. And by "what it really meant" I want to emphasize — what the change meant for the different social classes that composed Puerto Rican society. We can easily see, because it is abundantly documented, that the Puerto Rican propertied class welcomed the American invasion when it occurred with open arms. Every political spokesman of that class saw that invasion as bringing to Puerto Rico liberty, democracy, and progress, and as the prelude to the annexation of Puerto Rico by the richest and most powerful, and, we should remember, most "democratic," nation on earth. The subsequent disenchantment only occurred when the new imperial master made it clear that the invasion did not necessarily imply annexation, or the participation of the propertied class in the sumptuous banquet of the expanding American capitalist economy, but instead their colonial subordination to that economy.

It was then and only then that the "nationalism" of this class came into being. (Or rather to put it more exactly, the "nationalism" of the members of that class whose economic weakness made it impossible for them to profit from the new situation.) The well-known opposition of José de Diego, which is to say the opposition of the social class that he represented as President of the Chamber of Delegates, to the extending of American citizenship to Puerto Ricans, was founded on the categorical declaration by President Taft that citizenship did not necessarily pave the way for annexation or even the promise of annexation, as De Diego himself explained in a speech that all Puerto Rican independentists should read or reread. And when in addition it became clear that the new economic order, which is to say an economy based on cultivating sugar cane instead of one based on coffee, meant the ruin of the island's propertied class and the beginning of the independent participation of the working-class in the political life of the country, the "patriotic" rhetoric of the property owners reached such heights of demagoguery that not even the liberal professionals hesitated to ridicule and condemn it. Only in this context can we explain the virulent attacks by Rosendo Matienzo Cintrón, Nemesio Canales, and Luis Lloréns Torres on the "anti-imperialist" tirades of José de Diego, the wealthy lawyer of the Guánica sugar mill turned thundering *"Caballero de la Raza"* ("Knight-Errant of his People").

(And directly related to this last point, let me here add a long parenthesis on a subject so relevant that I find I cannot leave it out. Criticism of the political behavior of an historical figure of José de Diego's importance — and "to criticize is not to censure but rather to exercise the critical faculty," as José Martí used to say — should be interpreted as an effort, in the spirit of devotion to historical accuracy, to understand and pin down the reasons which determined the behavior of a whole sector of Puerto Rican society at a given moment. This behavior has been subject for half a century to the myth-making propensities of that sector's social and ideological heirs, and those of us who reply, or seek to reply, on behalf of the historical interests of the *other* Puerto Rican social class, the working class, shouldn't try to combat those earlier myths by inventing new myths. And *that*, unfortunately, as it seems to me, is what those two admirable researchers into Puerto Rican social history, Juan Flores and Ricardo Campos, have done in their essay entitled "Migración y cultura nacional puertorriqueños: perspectivas proletarias."* What Flores and Campos do in this essay is to contrast the mythical figure of the reactionary leader José de Diego with another mythical figure, the distinguished agitator and proletarian ideologue Ramón Romero Rosa. But had Flores and Campos borne in mind the fact that saints belong to religion and not to politics they would not have suppressed the fact that Romero Rosa, after giving great service to the Puerto Rican working class, wound up by joining the Unionist Party, which as we all know was the party of the opposing class. Flores and Campos obviously have no lack of pertinent information to explain all this and it is precisely for that reason that their essay, very much worth attending to in every other respect, falls into a certain Manichaeism which is at odds with the essential justice of their argument. But to return to my subject. . . .)

The Puerto Rican working class for its part also warmly welcomed the American invasion, but for very different reasons than those that had at the same time encouraged the property-owners. For what the workers saw in the arrival of the Americans was an opportunity for an all-out *settling of scores* with the property-owning class on all fronts, and on the cultural front, which is the one that now immediately concerns us, this settling of scores has been the motive force for all the cultural changes in Puerto Rican society from 1898 until our own day. The often-denounced American cultural penetration of Puerto Rico has of course been a fact and I should be the last to deny it. But I refuse to agree that this penetration amounts to a "transculturation," which is to say to an "Americanization" understood as a "de-Puerto Ricanization," in the whole of our society. Furthermore, I am

---

*Included in *Puerto Rico: identidad nacional y classes sociales* (*Coloquio de Princeton*), Ediciones Huracán, Río Piedras, 1979.

convinced that the causes and consequences of this penetration can only be fully understood in the context of the struggle, which in fact is only one aspect of the class struggle at the heart of our national society, between the "two cultures" of Puerto Rico.

The so-called "Americanization" of Puerto Rico has had two dialectically linked aspects. On the one hand it has obeyed *from without* an imperialist policy aimed at integrating Puerto Rican society into the American capitalist system as a dependent; but on the other hand it has corresponded *from within* to the struggle of the Puerto Rican masses against the hegemony of the property-owning class. The cultural achievements of this latter class under the Spanish colonial regime had, for reasons we have already explained, a liberal-bourgeois cast; but the new relation between social classes under the American regime obliged the property-owning class, marginated and expropriated by American capitalism, to abandon the liberalism of the professionals in that same class and to struggle for the conservation of its own cultural values. The cult of the land characteristic of the literature that the Puerto Rican élite has produced in this century no longer expresses, as is generally taught in literature courses in our university, a disinterested and lyrical sensibility moved by the beauties of our tropical landscape; what in fact it expresses is a very specific and historically-determined nostalgic longing for a lost land — and not land in either a symbolic or a metaphorical but in a literal sense, as the medium for material production now in the hands of foreigners. In other words, those who could no longer continue "doing the rounds of the farm" astride the traditional horse now devoted themselves to "doing the rounds" astride a *décima,* short story, or novel. And, stretching the metaphor only a little, with the same patriarchal spirit as in "the good old days," they substituted for the work force of peons and sharecroppers a work force consisting of — their own readers!

What nonetheless complicates matters is the fact that at the time of the American invasion a very important part of the landowning class in Puerto Rico consisted not so much of Puerto Ricans as of Spaniards, Corsicans, Majorcans, Catalans, and so on. All these landowners were seen by the Puerto Rican masses for what they were: foreigners and exploiters. It was precisely this social world that the three protagonists of *Los soles truncos* longed for, idealizing that world to the point of mythification. And to pass off this world as the world of "Puerto Ricanness," at grips with "American adulteration," not only constitutes a flagrant misrepresentation of the historical truth but also (and this is truly serious) an aggression against the Puerto Ricanness of the popular masses, whose ancestors, in many cases within living memory, lived in that world as slaves, squatters, or peons. Hence, just as the cultural values of the property-owning class helped them to resist "Americanization," so that same "Americanization" has helped the masses to oppose and supplant the cultural values of the property-owning class. But it helped not only the popular masses (and I think this should be emphasized) but also certain very important elements of that same property-owning class oppressed from within their own class, particularly women. For who can deny that the women's liberation movement in Puerto Rico, essentially progressive and just, in spite of any limitations that can be alleged against it, has been in very great measure the result of the "Americanization" of Puerto Rican society?

The prevailing ignorance or underestimation of these realities has had a baleful consequence: the idea put forward and spread by the traditional independence movement, that independence is necessary to protect and shore up a national cultural identity that the Puerto Rican masses have never felt as *their* true identity. Why have these advocates of independence been accused again and again of wanting to "return to the Spanish era?" Why have poor Puerto Ricans and black Puerto Ricans been conspicuous by their absence from the ranks of the traditional independence movement, whereas they have flocked into the populist annexationist movement? The traditional independence movement has usually answered the last question by saying that black Puerto Ricans who support annexation have become "alienated" as a result of colonialism. And their reasoning runs as follows: if black Puerto Ricans wish to become part of a racist society like that of the United States, then such an "aberration" can only be explained as a symptom of alienation.

However, those who reason thus either don't know or have forgotten an elementary historical truth: the experience of racism of Puerto Rican blacks came not from American, but from Puerto Rican society. In other words, those who have discriminated against blacks *in Puerto Rico* haven't been Americans, but white Puerto Ricans, many of whom moreover have always taken conspicuous pride in their foreign ancestry (Spanish, Catalan, Majorcan, etc.). What a Puerto Rican black, or for that matter what any poor Puerto Rican, even a white (and everyone knows that there has always been a much higher proportion of poor people among the blacks than whites) understands by "returning to the Spanish era" is this: returning to a society in which the white and property-owning part of the population has always oppressed and despised the non-white and non-property-owning part. For in fact how many black or poor Puerto Ricans could ever participate, even as simple voters, in Puerto Rican political life throughout the Spanish era? To be a voter in those days one had to be a property-owner or a taxpayer as well as knowing how to read and write, and how many black

Puerto Ricans, or poor Puerto Ricans of any sort, could meet those requirements?

And we won't even mention what it cost a black man to become a political *leader*. There is Barbosa, of course — but who else? And then it wasn't just plain Barbosa, it was *Doctor* Barbosa. And where did Barbosa study medicine? Not in Puerto Rico, where Spain never permitted the founding of a university, nor in Spain itself, where Puerto Rican students were invariably the sons of landowners or white professionals, but in the United States, more specifically in Michigan, a northern state with an old abolitionist tradition — all of which easily explains many of the things that the traditional supporters of independence may never have been able to understand about Barbosa and his annexationism. So that, in short, if the traditional Puerto Rican independence movement this century has been — in political, social, and cultural terms — a conservative ideology, engaged in the defense of the values of the old propertied class, then why on earth blame "alienation" for the failure of the masses to support that independence movement? Who have been and really still are the "alienated" in a true historical sense?

But when we turn to popular culture we have to admit that this culture, too, has in the course of its historical development seldom been homogeneous. For the first and much of the second hundred years of colonial life the mass of laborers, both in the countryside and in the towns, was concentrated near the coasts, most of them being black or mulatto and with a preponderance of slaves over free men. Later this proportion became inverted and freed blacks and mulattos outnumbered slaves until the abolition of slavery in 1873 formally put an end to the latter's inferior status. The earliest popular culture in Puerto Rico was therefore basically Afro-Antillean. The white *campesinado*, which came into being at a later date and then mainly in the mountainous central region of the island, produced a variant of the popular culture which developed in a relatively autonomous way, until the decline in coffee production in the mountains coinciding with the boom in sugar production in the coastal plains caused a major population shift from the "uplands" to the "lowlands." From that point on the two currents of the popular culture flowed into one channel, but with a clear predominance of the Afro-Antillean current, for demographic, social, and economic reasons.

The conservative marginated landowners, however, misrepresented these new social realities in their own literary production, proclaiming that the popular culture of the white peasantry was *the* popular culture par excellence. The literary *"jibarismo"* of the élite has been nothing else at bottom than that class's statement of its own racial and social prejudice. And so in the Puerto Rico of our own day, where the *jíbaro* has virtually ceased to have any demographic, economic, or cultural significance, the myth of the Puerto Rican as essentially a *jíbaro* stubbornly survives — whenever the old conservative élite, whether openly or covertly racist, sets pen to paper. And this at a time when it is really the proletarian Puerto Rican of mixed race who increasingly typifies popular society!

In short, each time the ideological spokesmen for the old conservative élite accuse the Puerto Rican popular masses of "alienation," "unawareness," or "loss of identity," all they are doing is to betray their own lack of confidence and their own alienation from those who, little though some people like having to admit it, constitute the immense majority of Puerto Ricans. What is more, those ideological spokesmen have done something equally negative and counter-productive: they have convinced many foreigners of good will, who are sympathetic to our independence, that the Puerto Rican people are the object of "cultural genocide." A particularly sad victim of this "anti-imperialist" propaganda, which is really nothing but the swan-song of a dying social class, has been the outstanding Cuban revolutionary poet Nicolás Guillén, whose "Canción puertorriqueña," as ill-informed as it is well-intentioned, has spread around the world the image of a culturally hybrid people capable of expressing themselves only in a ridiculous stutter of English and Spanish. All Puerto Ricans, whether supporters of independence or not, know that this vision of the cultural situation in Puerto Rico bears no relation whatsoever to the truth. And there are so many good reasons to justify Puerto Rico's independence that one cannot forgive an attempt to justify it by a reason that is patently false.

In my view, the good cultural reason for supporting independence is that independence is absolutely necessary to protect, orient, and secure the full development of Puerto Rico's true national identity, the identity that has its roots in that popular culture which the independence movement — if it *really* aspires to represent the authentic national will in this country — must understand and espouse without conditions or scruples born of distrust or prejudice. What is really happening in Puerto Rico today is the spectacular and irrevocable disintegration of that *fourth storey* which an advanced American capitalism and an opportunistic Puerto Rican populism began to build onto the island's social structure from the 1940s on. The patent collapse of the idea of the *Estado Libre Asociado* or Commonwealth, clearly demonstrates, if we view it from what seems to me the right historical perspective, that American colonialism, after sponsoring widespread economic transformations fundamentally in order to satisfy the needs of an expansionist imperialist economy at home, thereby creating a very real modernization-within-dependency in Puerto Rican society, can now only lead this society into a dead-end street and into a generalized malaise, whose rightly alarming symptoms are everywhere to be seen: massive unemployment and margination, a demoralizing dependency on a false generosity from abroad an uncontrollable upsurge in delinquency and criminality, to a great extent of foreign provenance, a disenchantment with politics and civic irresponsibility resulting from institutionalized demagoguery, and a whole Pandora's box of social ills that you know better than I, since you must live with them every day.

But to speak of the *present* bankruptcy of the colonial regime in no way implies that such a regime was a "good" regime until recently and only now becomes "bad." What I am trying to say — and it matters a great deal to me not to be misunderstood — is that the eighty years of American domination in Puerto Rico represent the history of a political and economic undertaking whose immediate stages were viable *as they occurred,* but which were inevitably doomed, as indeed is any historical undertaking based on colonial dependency, to founder *in the long run* into the state of *un*viability in which we are now living. This unviability of the colonial regime is precisely what for the first time in our history makes national independence viable. And not merely viable, but also, as I have just argued, absolutely necessary.

Those of us both from within and without our country committed to a socialist future for Puerto Rico have before us the daunting task of neither more nor less than the total reconstruction of Puerto Rican society. (And when I speak of "a socialist future for Puerto Rico" I speak, as you should already know, of a *democratic* socialism, pluralist and independent, which is the only socialism worthy of the name, and not of that other "socialism" which is bureaucratic, monolithic, and authoritarian, and instituted *in the name* only of the working class by a new ruling class one can only call a state bourgeoisie, since it is the real proprietor of the means of production, held by virtue of the at once immovable and all-powerful "apparatus" of the State.) My well-known disagreement with the traditional independence movement in this respect is a disagreement between two conceptions of the historical aims of such a reconstruction of Puerto Rican society. I do not believe in reconstructing backward, to a past bequeathed us by Spanish colonialism and an old élite irrevocably condemned by history. I believe instead in reconstructing forward, toward a future as defined by the best proletarian socialists in Puerto Rico early in this century when they advocated a national independence capable of organizing the country into "an industrial democracy governed by the workers"; toward a future which, basing itself on the cultural tradition of the popular masses, will rediscover and redeem the essentially *Caribbean* nature of our collective identity and thereby acknowledge, once and for all, that the natural destiny of Puerto Rico is identical to that of all the other Caribbean peoples, whether they hail from the islands or from the mainland.

In this sense I conceive the national independence of all these peoples as merely a prerequisite — albeit the indispensable prerequisite — for achieving a great confederation that will definitively unite us in a just, effective joint organization at the economic, political and cultural levels. Only by means of such an organization may we take our rightful place within the greater communities of Latin America and the world. In economic matters, far from being merely an utopian wish, such unity is an objective necessity. In political matters, it answers to a manifest historical imperative, which is the liquidation of our common colonial past by establishing popular and non-capitalist regimes. And in cultural matters, which is what now specifically concerns us, it is essential for us so that we may recognize and *assume* a reality that even the most concerned among us have consistently ignored.

Hitherto, the fact that the Caribbean peoples speak several different European languages instead of just one has been seen as a factor in our disunity — and as a factor in our disunity it has been used against us by those various imperialisms which have claimed to speak in our name. But should we then, the subjugated, regard linguistic diversity from the same viewpoint as they, the subjugators? On the contrary, we should see this diversity as a unifying and uniting factor, since it is a consequence of our shared history. The great community of the Caribbean is multilingual. This is both true and irreversible and as such it should serve less to fragment and defeat than to stimulate and enrich us. Seen in this light American imperialism, thanks to one of those "sly tricks of history" that philosophers refer to, has imposed on us Puerto Ricans a mastery of English — but without making us forget Spanish, my dear Nicolás Guillén! — only (and unintentionally) to make it easier for us to draw into closer alliance with our English-speaking brothers of the Caribbean.

We Puerto Ricans have to learn English, not as the route to cultural suicide whereby we become dissolved into the turbulent mainstream of American life, assimilated to that "brutal and unruly North that so despises us," to quote José Martí, but so that we may with greater ease and profit integrate ourselves into that rich Caribbean world to which we belong by historical necessity. When finally Puerto Rico becomes independent within a great confederacy of independent nations — mestizo, popular and democratic — not only will we then be able and willing to appreciate and protect our national language, the good Spanish of Puerto Rico, as we should; we will also be able and willing to institute the teaching of English and French in our schools (with particular emphasis on local dialects), not as the languages of empire, but as languages at the service of our complete and final decolonization.

(1979)

Literature and National Identity in Puerto Rico

The *Aguinaldo Puertorriqueño* of 1843, a book that Salvador Brau once called "the first infant cry of the Puerto Rican muse," was, according to its nine young authors, intended to be "an entirely indigenous work, advantageously ridding our culture of the marzipan, the *antigua botella de Jerez* or old-fashioned bottle of sherry, and the vulgar Christmas verses [that have hitherto characterized it]." In the climate of today's nationalism, grounded as it is on the virtues of the native and indigenous, it seems a paradox that the young authors of the *Aguinaldo* should have rejected, not only Hispanic features that the new creole mentality was beginning to find alien (the "marzipan," the *antigua botella de Jerez*), but also something that seems to us eminently characteristic of the native and indigenous ("the vulgar Christmas verses"). But in fact this paradox is more apparent than real and can be resolved into a highly coherent proposition once we analyze it in the light of the social history of Puerto Rico.

Let me first draw your attention to three words in the passage just quoted, that in my opinion provide a key to its meaning. Two of these words come straight from the authors of the *Aguinaldo: antigua,* or old fashioned, and "vulgar." We have seen that the first of these refers to the bottle of sherry, but *antigua* isn't merely a synonym for *old,* since it also carries the suggestion of *worn out.* (To quote a well-known example, just think of the phrase *ancien régime,* with all this implies of a social and political system superceded by something more modern.) The other key word used by the authors of the *Aguinaldo* is "vulgar," referring to the *coplas* or verses of popular origin composed extemporaneously at Christmas-time. I have spoken elsewhere[1] of "young writers who were literary spokesmen for an incipient national bourgeoisie and who viewed 'popular culture' with the understandable disdain of a social class just beginning to feel superior to the rest of their compatriots, despite lingering feelings of inferiority toward the metropolis. Perhaps we should now confront the fact that our national literature was founded by young gentlemen, or as the vernacular has it, *blanquitos*.[2] At the time, nonetheless, these *blanquitos* represented not only the most progressive, but indeed the *only* sector of Puerto Rican society that could challenge a colonial dependency in cultural matters. Their rejection of the 'popular' really expressed a determination to rub shoulders with Spanish writers in the field of cultivated literature." I still think this interpretation fundamentally valid, even though it needs further elaboration. But before we begin to elaborate, we should first examine the third key term used, not by the writers of 1843, but by myself, namely "new" as applied to the creole mentality of the young authors of the *Aguinaldo*.

Let us now analyze the three key terms, in the order given above. To say that the lads of 1843 used the term *antigua* to reject something they thought already moribund isn't something that I myself have belatedly discovered in this Year of our Lord 1978. In fact when the *Aguinaldo* first appeared an older writer, Francisco Vasallo, reacted in a very hostile manner, indicating that he clearly understood, even if he rejected, the young authors' modernizing intent and cosmopolitanism. "What you want to do," wrote Vasallo (a Spaniard resident in Puerto Rico), "is to imitate what people are doing in France, England and Germany." Notice that Vasallo uses the present tense: "what people *are* doing," not "what people *did*" or "have done." Given, then, what we know about the scarcity of books then in Puerto Rico — even forty years later Alejandro Tapia y Rivera was to complain about that scarcity! — and knowing too how few Puerto Ricans could travel to the countries mentioned by Vasallo, it is impossible to escape the conclusion that the modernizing cosmopolitanism Vasallo condemns could only have been the result of a transformation at the heart of Puerto Rican society.

And indeed such a transformation had in fact taken place, in about the fourth decade of the nineteenth century and as the direct result of an intimately inter-related series of historical events. The process (whose immediate and long-term antecedents aren't in fact relevant here) began with the Haitian revolt of 1804. Not only did this revolt end black slavery and ensure Haiti's national independence from France, it also ruined the Haitian sugar industry, then the most important in the Caribbean and one of the most important in the world. As a result, sugar became scarce and its price rose on the world market. The other European powers with Caribbean colonies were then faced with a great economic opportunity, the recovery of a market hitherto dominated by France, and with a grave social and political danger, the repetition in their own territories of the slave rebellions that had triumphed in Haiti. So as to encourage the first and avoid the second, the Spanish government radically modified its emigration policy for Puerto Rico, opening the island's doors by the *Real Cédula de Gracias* of 1815 to every white foreigner who could bring with him investment capital, technical knowledge for sugar production, or slaves. Immediately English, French, Dutch, German and Spanish immigrants flocked to Puerto Rico, together with creole refugees from those South American colonies fighting for their independence. What this wave of immigration meant for the eventual development of Puerto Rican society is a topic that, like so many others in our brief but complex history, awaits a detailed analysis to bring together into one synthesis its many varied aspects. However, in this essay I wish merely to point to certain of these aspects.

In the first place, it is more than reasonable to suppose that the main object of the immigration policy was to level out a certain "disequilibrium" in the island's population. This "disequilibrium" wasn't exactly quantitative: the figures of the 1812 census reveal an almost exact parity between the races (93,623 whites and 89,391 blacks and mulattos). In fact, it was rather qualitative, as the figures themselves reveal when examined in their proper context. Of the 89,391 non-white inhabitants, 71,855 were free and only 17,536 slaves. If we continue to subdivide these figures we discover that of the 71,855 non-white but free inhabitants, 58,983 were mulattos and only 12,872 blacks. But in addition, all the free blacks are listed as *agregados* or share-croppers, whereas the mulattos are not specifically included under this heading. This reveals a fundamental difference in the social status of blacks and free mulattos, with the latter being further advanced economically and therefore, we must assume, socially as well.

The mestizo's importance for Puerto Rican society throughout the second half of the eighteenth century (the historical period immediately preceding the promulgation of the *Cédula de Gracias*) is personified by two men whose representativeness has been practically ignored by Puerto Rican historians: the almost unknown Miguel Henríquez and the still poorly known José Campeche. About Miguel Henríquez, suffice it to say that he was a Spanish shoemaker who began his spectacular career as a *testaferro* or front man of the Spanish governor of the time in the lucrative business of smuggling. He received his privateer's license to prey on the English in the Caribbean and was so successful that he was decorated with the *Orden de la Real Efigie* and reached the rank of Captain, thus earning the right to be called "don." On his own he organized and led the expedition, composed mainly of free blacks from Cangrejos, that rescued the island of Vieques from the English. He became the richest man in Puerto Rico, owning an immense amount of land near San Juan, and the main economic prop of the civil and ecclesiastical administrations on the island. All this enormous power finally brought about his downfall. Accused and condemned by the Spanish authorities, he died a ruined man in circumstances that are still a mystery.

As for José Campeche, there is no lack of sound evidence as to the excellent formal quality of his painting, but the most important story, the significance of what this son of an *esclavo "coartado,"* or slave buying his liberty by installments, achieved in the Puerto Rican life of his times, remains to be told. Nor can we fully yet explain the more-or-less hidden social criticism that informs his work.

What may we conclude from all this except that by the end of the eighteenth century Puerto Rico's mulatto population was on the way to becoming something dangerously similar to what it soon did become in Haiti: the detonator for a rebellion of colored peoples against a government of whites? But there was an important difference in that in Puerto Rico the black population constituted a minority whereas in Haiti it constituted an overwhelming majority. And yet the much greater number of mulattos in Puerto Rico more than compensated for this disproportion in the black population, so who can then doubt that the main objective of the *Real Cédula de Gracias* of 1815 was to "whiten" Puerto Rican society so as to prevent what had happened in Haiti from happening here?[3] Obviously, it wasn't merely a matter of *quantitative* "whitening" at the base of the social pyramid, since in fact the *Cédula* had as one of its main objectives the strengthening of Puerto Rico's sugar industry and this of course necessitated an *increase* in the number of slaves in the work force. (In fact, several of the *Cédula's* provisions were specifically designed to make it *easier* to bring slaves to Puerto Rico.) No, what was really at stake was a *qualitative* "whitening" of the population, in other words a re-Europeanization of the white élite, whose relative weakness vis-à-vis the increasing power of the mulattos obviously gave the Spanish regime genuine cause for alarm. (If we had more space at our disposal we should feel obligated to compare the Puerto Rico of Henríquez and Campeche with the Puerto Rico of Ramón Power. Here is an eminently worthwhile subject, namely the existence of what with historical accuracy we may call the *three* Puerto Rican "fatherlands": the Puerto Rico of the blacks, the Puerto Rico of the mulattos, and the Puerto Rico of the white creoles. The joint integration of these three fatherlands into one true national fatherland isn't yet complete — indeed it could only *be* completed in a genuinely integrated society, which would be a society without social classes, without castes . . . and without all forms of bureaucratic despotism.)

The qualitative "whitening" of Puerto Rican society wasn't achieved by this first wave of immigrants, but by a second wave which arrived toward the middle of the century. But perhaps I should make it clear, if only to state the grounds for a conclusion I hope to come to later, that what this second wave of immigrants, consisting mostly of Corsicans and Majorcans, really represented was a second conquest and colonization for Puerto Rico. This time the conquered clearly weren't the Taino Indians, who had been exterminated three centuries previously as a result of the genocidal policies of the first conquerors, but rather the white *campesinos* of Puerto Rico's mountainous interior, who had been virtually out of touch with the urban and semi-urban cultures on the coasts. As a result of this new colonization the mountain-dwelling peasantry, the original *jíbaros*, were converted into *agregados*, or share-croppers, tied to the land by the institution of the *libreta* or pass-book — a telling example of how the objective needs of a society's economic development determine its legal instruments. Soon the region's prevailing subsistence economy was replaced by an economy based on large coffee plantations, depending on a stable work force that was forbidden to move from one part of the country to another.

This plantation economy was the economic mainstay of a new sector of the creole ruling class, a sector the most influential part of which benefited from its main crop's easy access to European markets for the rest of the century[4] and that created for itself, bit by bit and always in a subordinate relation to the more developed world of the coasts, a way of life or "culture" in the anthropological sense, founded on the seignorial values appropriate to its economic structure. Until 1898 this coffee-growing sector of the Puerto Rican ruling class invariably lagged behind, in cultural and social terms, the sugar-growing, commercial, and professional sectors of the coasts, and one has only to review the names of that period's intellectual figures (the overwhelming majority of whom came from the coastal regions and their immediate hinterland) to realize the very meagre contribution made by this coffee-growing class to the country's cultural activity. We will search the mountain regions in vain for figures like Alonso, Tapia, Acosta, Hostos, Betances, Gautier, Stahl, or Zeno. Whenever someone from "the uplands" like Muñoz Rivera succeeded in distinguishing himself, it was because he had already moved to the urban centers on the coast. However, after 1898 the newly settled creole hinterland, too, began to contribute important figures to our cultural patrimony — Lloréns Torres, Meléndez Muñoz, Oliver Frau — and it was the seignorial values of just these coffee-growing areas that increasingly nourished the thinking of those members of the Puerto Rican ruling class who lived on the coasts. But before we begin to explain this phenomenon it is necessary to go back and pick up the chronological thread of our argument.

We were saying that the first wave of immigrants didn't fully accomplish the qualitative "whitening" of Puerto Rican society. But what they *did* achieve — and it was decisive — was to postpone in Puerto Rico the eventual melding of the races into a predominantly Afro-Antillean society, as had already occurred in the English and French colonies. Their advent also frustrated the possibility that in Puerto Rico a biracial élite would come into being, with whites and mulattos sharing the privileges of a ruling class as in Santo Domingo. In Puerto Rico, by contrast, it was the immigrants and their descendants who soon formed the embryo of a ruling class, a class whose economic power, founded on the development of a sugar industry and on the commercial activity generated by that sugar industry, soon allowed it to dominate political life at the local level of municipalities, political districts, etc.[5] Puerto Rican historians this century have repeatedly pointed out the retrograde character of the influence exercised by most of these immigrants on the ideological aspects of social evolution, clearly because these immigrants had become so closely identified with the island's colonial institutions. But I know of no study that has gone into what these immigrants and their descendants have meant for the economic, political and cultural development of Puerto Rican society. Such a study would reveal in local terms the fulfilment of a universal law of history: that the attitudes of a social class are less determined by the circumstances of its origin than by its material interests at any specific historical moment. Conceived in the early years of the nineteenth century, the new ruling class[6] was in effect born under the sign of political conservatism and as it grew it soon came into conflict with the very colonial regime that had nurtured it. In due course the sons and grandsons of those conservative immigrants became the leaders of Puerto Rican liberalism. (The case of Salvador Brau, the son of an exiled Venezuelan woman and of a Catalan living in Puerto Rico, is one example among many.)

On the other hand, those historians who have drawn attention to the conservative ideology of the new immigrants haven't yet, to my knowledge, tried to answer the more fundamental question: what really *were* the historical results of the transformation of Puerto Rican society caused by these waves of immigration? Obviously this isn't merely a matter of vaguely speculating about what didn't happen, but of getting to the bottom of what did. And, as we have seen, what in fact happened was the racial and cultural "whitening" of the creole élite, thereby preventing the emergence in Puerto Rico of a predominantly Afro-Antillean society and a biracial élite. But — and this is one of those *buts* that is worth underlining — what wasn't eliminated, because it couldn't have been, was the existence of the black and mulatto majority in Puerto Rican society. These blacks and mulattos, historically speaking, constituted the cement of Puerto Rican nationality because they were the first to *feel* Puerto Rico as their true home and because they had no roots in or loyalty to Spain, Corsica, the Balearic Islands, or indeed anywhere else. After the "whitening" we have already referred to, they stayed put and grew in numbers, an oppressed and despised population at the heart of the young country and lorded over by people who were by comparison the newcomers.[7]

From 1898 on, the conditions created by a new economic set-up allowed this group to participate in social life in a way previously denied them under Spanish rule. The class struggles of the first decades of the twentieth century, determined by the development of a dependent capitalism in Puerto Rico, were also to a considerable extent struggles between castes, with profound racial overtones. For example, who of a certain age doesn't remember the way the creole bourgeoisie used to describe the workers' movement as *la negrada socialista* (that bunch of socialist niggers)? It is precisely in the fear and resentment experienced by the creole bourgeoisie, as a result of the blacks' and mulattos' improved status under the American colonial regime, that we may find an explanation for the implicit and explicit racism so prevalent in the literature written by the Puerto Rican élite this century.

But to return to the cultural results of the first wave of immigration: I should describe one result, and one that particularly interests me in the present context, as the creation of economic circumstances favorable for the flowering of a literature that (as was to be expected) embodied an upper-class point of view. The expansion of the Puerto Rican economy gave rise, among other things, to the development of the periodical press, virtually the cradle of our literature. The same economic development made it possible for upper-class creole students to attend metropolitan universities. And we should bear in mind that the second book in our national literature, the *Album Puertorriqueño* of 1844, was the work of a group of Puerto Rican students in Barcelona entitled the "Grupito Criollo" (Little Creole Group). One member of this group was Manuel A. Alonso, future author of *El gíbaro*, and it was Alonso who published in the *Album* a sonnet entitled "El puertorriqueño," which is intended to give a physical and moral description of our creole identity.

> Color moreno, frente despejada,
> Mirar lánguido, altivo y penetrante,
> La barba negra, pálido el semblante,
> Rostro enjuto, nariz proporcionada.

Mediana talla, marcha acompasada;
El alma de ilusiones anhelante,
Agudo ingenio, libre y arrogante,
Pensar inquieto, mente acalorada;

Humano, afable, justo, dadivoso,
En empresas de amor siempre variable,
Tras la gloria y placer siempre afanoso,

Y en amor a su patria insuperable,
Este es, a no dudarlo, fiel diseño
Para copiar un buen Puertorriqueño.[8]

About this sonnet I have on another occasion written the
following: "The reference at the beginning of the sonnet to
'dark in color' shouldn't be misinterpreted, since what it
refers to is a *white* Puerto Rican whose skin has been tanned
by the tropical sun (as the 'pale' complexion and a 'well-
proportioned nose' confirm). The 'country,' subject of an
'unsurpassable love,' is obviously no longer Spain, but Puerto
Rico. The 'soul tremulous with dreams,' the wit that is 'free
and proud,' the 'restless thought' and the 'ardent mind,'
speak of an inquisitive and challenging attitude toward
reality. In fact, the portrait is of a social class as a whole:
the new creole bourgeoisie already conscious of its historical
destiny."[9]

To these comments I now wish to add the following: when
Alonso wrote his sonnet, one out of every two inhabitants of
Puerto Rico wasn't white and approximately one out of every
ten was a slave. And matters hadn't changed much five
years later when Alonso published *El gíbaro*, a book that in
no way reflects the true racial composition of Puerto Rican
society. What is more, it doesn't even primarily deal with
the Puerto Rican *campesino* of Alonso's time, as students, to

their astonishment, only discover once they get past the title
(a reference not to the subject-matter of the book but to the
author's pseudonym, "El gíbaro de Caguas"). And yet, most
Puerto Rican literary historians continue to refer to *El gíbaro*
as the first literary expression of our national identity![10]
But I am convinced that this so-called "national identity" is
nothing more than the identity of the educated members of
the country's ruling class. Alonso was of course himself a
liberal and the representative of a class then historically on
the rise which found itself in opposition to the most conservative elements in the larger society to which it belonged, but
the problem was that this liberalism of Alonso's was fatally
limited, at least as far as the notion of "national identity"
was concerned, by the brutal and determining fact that fully
half of his compatriots (although probably he wouldn't
have called them "compatriots") were either slaves or the
descendants of slaves. And if on the one hand the cholera
epidemic of 1855 was soon to decimate the slave population,
even more significant on the other was the institution in
1849, the year *El gíbaro* was published, of the regimen of the
libreta or pass-book, a measure which would soon convert a
large proportion of the free population, including the white
day-laborers, into virtual serfs tied to the land. That these
people had as distinct a sense of their identity as did the
slaves and their descendants is unquestionable, but in default
of a written literature, that they were obviously in no condition to produce, we have to search for expressions of this
identity in the diverse manifestations of popular culture.
And the fact that *El gíbaro*, which as we all know is a
collection of vignettes of popular life, throws so little light
on the existence of the country's black and mulatto popula-
tions, reveals the fundamental truth, that Alonso's class
wasn't yet capable of extending its own sense of a Puerto
Rican identity to include those large sectors of the
population that constituted the country's real social

base.[11] For that reason it would be quite inappropriate to refer to a truly developed concept of national class identity at this first stage of the development of Puerto Rican literature.

Assuming what I have just said to be correct, we must now recognize that this state of affairs, insofar as it relates to our subject, continued without any essential change until the end of the century. The year *El gíbaro* was published Alejandro Tapia y Rivera was twenty-three years old and had already written his first play, the historical drama *Roberto D'Evreux*. The flagrant romanticism of this play is evidence of that determination to "imitate what they are doing in France, England and Germany" that Francisco Vasallo had imputed to the young authors of the *Aguinaldo* in 1843. However, it is somewhat revealing that for the contemporaries of Alonso and Tapia it was *Roberto D'Evreux* and not *El gíbaro* that marked the beginnings of Puerto Rican literature. Soon after Tapia's death,[12] Manuel Zeno Gandía and Rafael del Valle stated the following in a letter published in 1882: "Whatever posterity may decide about the value of his works, no one will be able to deny that Tapia has the glory of being the founder of Puerto Rican literature." Why twentieth-century students of this literature have taken this honor from Tapia and awarded it to Alonso is something important that now needs to be explained.

There is no justification for giving Alonso the priority on chronological grounds, since *Roberto D'Evreux* antedates *El gíbaro* by two years. Whereas Alonso's work belongs to the side of romanticism that deals with customs and manners, the so-called *costumbrista* side, Tapia's play clearly belongs to the cosmopolitan side of romanticism, *Roberto D'Evreux* being a dramatization of the love affair between England's Queen Elizabeth I and the Earl of Essex. What is more, whereas, as Salvador Brau has pointed out, Alonso shows the influence of the Spaniard Bréton de los Herreros, other critics have noted stylistic resemblances between *Roberto D'Evreux* and certain works of German romanticism. In other words, what we have here are two literary spokesmen for the same social class, the incipient creole bourgeoisie of the mid-nineteenth century. Alonso was traditional and *costumbrista*, Tapia modernizing and cosmopolitan. For his (younger) contemporaries Zeno Gandía and Del Valle, it was Tapia who was "the founder of Puerto Rican literature" in a way that was "undeniable," but for twentieth-century literary historians such as Antonio S. Pedreira and F. Manrique Cabrera, the founder of the national literature was just as categorically Alonso.

Let us pause for a moment over this strange discrepancy. First we should bear in mind, to keep things in perspective, that Zeno and Del Valle, like Pedreira and Cabrera, based their opinions on *all* of Tapia's oeuvre. This of course includes the regionalist novel *Cofresí*, together with novels critical of country ways such as *Póstumo el transmigrado* and its sequel *Póstumo el envirginado*; it also includes plays of social concern such as *La cuarterona* and *La parte del león*, not to mention Tapia's biographical essays on two distinguished Puerto Ricans, José Campeche and Ramón Power. To all this we should add the *Biblioteca histórica de Puerto Rico*, which Tapia played a leading part in compiling and editing, a book that Pedreira, Cabrera and all their contemporaries knew and were proud of, as an expression of the historical consciousness attained by the mid-nineteenth-century intellectual élite. (The Institute of Puerto Rican Culture brought out the second edition of this work in 1945 on the initiative of its then president, the essayist Vicente Géigel Polanco.)

To these we should also add *Mis Memorias* (published forty-five years after Zeno and Del Valle gave their opinions on Tapia[13] but cited by Pedreira in *Insularismo* and by Cabrera in *Historia de la literatura puertorriqueña*), a book in which Tapia harshly condemns the negative aspects of the society in which he lives. His condemnation of slavery shows a perception of the consequences of this system *for the whole of Puerto Rican society* that is conspicuously absent in the writings of many Puerto Rican historians and sociologists today. As Tapia says: "It won't come as a surprise that backwardness and other social ills are endemic in a society which has for so long depended on an institution such as slavery, something that has sapped men's energies and undermined their characters merely by forcing them to accommodate to its demands."[14] And a few paragraphs further on: "My compatriots are sick. Moral inertia, indifference, and egotism devour them. A few people condemn these faults, but without knowing how to remedy them. Rather more people recognize the faults, but are content merely to complain; what they don't understand is that the most important reform, which they long for but won't act on, is necessarily self-reform," (*ibid.*, p. 90). How could two writers such as Zeno Gandía and Rafael del Valle *not* have seen Tapia as the true founder of Puerto Rican literature — Zeno Gandía, the future author of the novels comprising "the chronicle of a sick world," and Del Valle, so rebellious a figure that he had to suffer a seven-year exile that only ended with the termination of Spanish rule in the island? Neither of them needed to have *read Mis Memorias* to know Tapia and his ideas, since these were ideas that they themselves shared.[15]

Why then do the best known twentieth-century scholars of Puerto Rican literature, scholars well versed in Tapia's work, persist in citing Alonso as "the founder of Puerto Rican literature?" I think this can best be understood as the result of an ideological displacement that intellectuals in the creole ruling class suffered as the result of the change of sovereignty in Puerto Rico from Spain to the United States.

As I have argued elsewhere,[16] the creole bourgeoisie under Spanish rule was a social class on the historical rise and as such, receptive to the most advanced trends in contemporary thought. However, under American rule an important sector of this class, including most of the intellectuals, began very soon to suffer the effects of a marginalization caused by the growth of a new absentee capitalism. When their class was on the rise historically, the intellectuals of the creole bourgeoisie formed the habit of looking to the future and toward the change and progress they had themselves initiated, with the result that the best nineteenth-century literature in Puerto Rico is characterized by a progressive and innovative spirit. But in the subsequent period of marginalization and crisis the intellectuals of that same class felt they had to look to the past, to what they were losing and making every effort to preserve, and as a result they produced a literature that was essentially conservative. (Virtually all our critics and literary historians persist in describing this literature as *the* national literature, but we should remember that in the first decades of the present century a workers' literature inspired by the ideals of socialism came into being, the importance of which has been sufficiently emphasized by other speakers in this Colloquium.[17])

It is to the easily explained conservatism of the Puerto Rican cultural élite this century that we must attribute the ideological misreading of *El gíbaro* by the critics of the Generation of the 1930s. In reality, Alonso wasn't what Pedreira, Cabrera, *et al* said he was — which of course isn't to say that *everything* they say about Alonso misses the mark. For example, when Pedreira states that "with the appearance of Alonso the soul of Puerto Rico finally declares itself"[18] it is clear that he is defining a "national soul" in terms of the cultural nationalism of 1934 rather than in terms of the regionalist liberalism of 1849. The same applies to

Cabrera's remark that Alonso's new subject-matter was "nothing less than the live substance that gives a convincing outline to his people's soul."[19] Of course, Cabrera doesn't go to the extreme that Pedreira does (albeit "preserving a due sense of proportion") when the latter compares the modest *Gíbaro* with the *Poema del Cid* and *Martín Fierro.* Still, Cabrera's excited discovery of "his people's soul" in Alonso's book no doubt answers the same need to *recuperate* the past as the work of the other intellectuals of the creole bourgeoisie, faced this century by a process of social, economic, political — and so ultimately cultural — change that can only presage their margination, or even disappearance, as a class.

The truth is that Alonso not only does not recognize the essence or outlines of a "national soul" in the way of life of the Puerto Rican peasantry of his time, he sees and criticizes that way of life as backward and primitive. But let me repeat now what I have already written elsewhere: "The writer knows that the rural world that peoples his pages is in process of disappearing. 'We are moving through a period of transition,' he says, 'in which the old is vanishing and the new is arriving to replace it.' And he doesn't bewail this, because one of the pillars of his liberal upbringing, and one of the traits of his status as a spokesman for a bourgeoisie on the rise, is his love of progress. He writes his book to record a reality that is disappearing, rather than to lament its disappearance."[20] Those who will lament the disappearance of that reality will be its interpreters in the following century, consciously creating an ideology of things past and gone, i.e., *jibarismo* or cult of the *jíbaro,* to oppose the imagined virtues of an idealized past to the real or imagined evils of a present, characterized (among other things) by the destruction of many of the traditional values of a now marginalized creole bourgeoisie.

An ideologized re-reading was much more easily applied to Alonso than to Tapia because Tapia's work, much richer, more complex and more problematical than Alonso's, had already challenged some of those traditional values of the creole bourgeoisie, such as (among others) a Catholic orthodoxy in religious matters, power and prestige based on wealth, and the superiority of men to women and of whites to blacks — as well as having undertaken the advocacy and defense of many of the changes the modernizing dynamic of the American colonial regime was soon to impose upon Puerto Rican society.[21] Pedreira's inability to understand that Tapia's cosmopolitanism was in its historical context the expression of his progressive modernity led him to see in Tapia's work a proof that "generally speaking, Puerto Rican literature builds its castles in the air." And he adds, "Tapia's most important plays and novels do not have the distinctive flavor of our own biology and geography."[22] Indeed, not even a story like "El loco de Sanjuanópolis" could make Pedreira see that Puerto Rican biology and geography weren't for Tapia mere pretexts for a light-hearted folkloric romp, but rather the starting-points for speculative flights that were extraordinarily progressive at the time. As for "biology," what is one to say about Tapia's very advanced notions (always, of course, in the context of his own era) about women's rights, as compared, say, to the reactionary anti-feminism shown by Pedreira in his *Insularismo*? In this respect Pedreira was doomed to a more genuine ideological limbo than the presumed geographical and biological limbos, where, without any real understanding, he placed Tapia.

"My compatriots are sick," Tapia had written shortly before his death in 1882. "Chronicles of a sick world" was to be the general title of the cycle of realist novels that Manuel Zeno Gandía began with the publication of *La Charca* a decade later.[23] Today, the Puerto Rican reader is used to having *El gíbaro* extolled this century as the eponymous hero of national identity, so he is bound to be surprised at Zeno's opinion of the *campesinos* of his own day in *La Charca*: "a mountain rabble," "a bloodless crew," "a bunch of anemic beings without any clear idea of what was really wrong with them," "a mountain mob [who] wasted their time in foolish pleasures and in stupid entertainment. . . ." Their customs provoked Zeno to judgments that flatly contradict the enthusiastic encomia of *criollista* prose writers and essayists of the succeeding generations: "their songs are of an admirable sonority and cadence, but the lyrics are nonsensical"; "the monotonous sing-song of a country bard who declaimed his incoherent *décimas* amid the coarse laughter and gibes of the assembled throng"; "the sounds pulsated through the air and stirred up feverish agitation in a paralytic people . . . like the sorrowing sighs of a dying people, who, laughing and singing, sink ever more deeply into abjection."

As for the fighting cocks that the most celebrated poets of lyric patriotism were to praise with such nativist fervor in later years, Zeno sees them with a very different focus born of his progressivist positivism: "They were utterly deformed. Their neck and tail feathers had been trimmed and in that ridiculous nakedness the birds look both odd and repulsive." In this same context it is worth pointing out that Zeno, in all 250 pages of *La Charca*, never once uses the word *jíbaro*. Without a doubt his attitude is closely related to that disdain for the "vulgar Christmas verses" expressed by the young authors of the *Aguinaldo Puertorriqueño* of 1843 and to that sense of "old ways that are now disappearing" that Manuel Alonso refers to, without a trace of nostalgia, in *El gíbaro*. In any event, it certainly wasn't the Puerto Rican *campesinos* that Zeno saw as the personification of national identity.

This vision of Puerto Rico as a sick and helpless society, characteristic of progressive Puerto Rican nineteenth-century intellectuals, achieved its most radical expression in Eugenio María de Hostos. When Hostos, the most cultured Puerto Rican of his day, returned to the island in 1898 just after the American invasion, his eyes rested with anguish on a heart-rending reality: "The island's population," he wrote, "is totally impoverished. Physiological and economic misery go hand in hand. Malarial fever, that turns the individual into a mummy, is also mummifying the whole of society. These barely-moving skeletons on the coastal plains and in the mountains, who give proof of how systematic the colonial regime has been in its policy of *mass relocations*;[24] that sicklied childhood; that sunken-chested adolescence; that spoiled manhood; that premature old age; in short, that individual and social debility everywhere to be seen — all this seems to have rendered our people incapable of helping themselves."[25] And, as if echoing Tapia's criticism of those who are "content merely to complain" even though they know what is wrong, Hostos made it clear that it wasn't just the popular masses who were to be found in this state of utter prostration but also the intellectual élite, from whom so much more was then to be expected: "They are so corrupted by colonization that not even the most cultivated men in Puerto Rico ... can make up their minds to take any sort of initiative, either by summoning up their own energies, or by ceasing to hope that those in power will do it all for them" (*op. cit.*, p. 13).

The *Disquisiciones sociológicas* of Salvador Brau, written between 1882 and 1886, simultaneously provide a diagnosis of the Puerto Rican social malaise, a defense of those victims unjustly blamed for causing their own ills, and a resumé of the appropriate remedies to alleviate the general misery. Two passages from *Las clases jornaleras de Puerto Rico* (1882) will suffice to give the gist of Brau's sociological thought.

Referring to "the daily sustenance of our poor laborers," he says:

> It is obvious that such insufficient nutrition can in no way counterbalance the influences of a burning climate and of work that is both arduous and unrelenting. This causes the poverty of the blood, the lack of muscular development, and the sicklied and emaciated look that so strike Europeans when they reach these shores. But even though it may be true that no one has bothered to tell these people the advantages that would accrue to them from a form of nutrition richer in natural juices, one may still question whether such admonitions would do any good, since the quality of their nutrition has inevitably to depend upon what they earn. . . . If their earnings were greater, there is no doubt that their daily nutrition would prove less niggardly.[26]

And further on he writes:

> It cannot be denied that the laboring classes on our island not only lack a moral education, but even the training necessary for the tasks they do to earn a living. The day-laborers haven't a notion of the most rudimentary theories of agronomics; the different phases of the moon and the periodic movement of the tides are for them, as for virtually all small rural landowners, the sacred text of their beliefs. They know nothing about the need for fertilizer; the classification of soils; the importance of trees; the deadly effects of marshland; the need to irrigate crops; the way machines can increase productive efforts a hundredfold; the use of certain herbs and plants for industrial, scientific, or merely hygenic needs; the improvement of crops by selecting or grafting different

short nothing that isn't routine, empirical and full of
error. . . . Indeed, how could one expect our countrymen
ever to know about such matters, since no one has ever
taken the trouble to teach them? (*ibid.*, pp. 177–179)

It is worth asking after all this just what the national
identity (that national identity that some Puerto Rican
writers this century have so zealously tried to track back
into the nineteenth century) could have meant for men like
Alonso, Tapia, Hostos, Brau and Zeno. To my knowledge,
none of them posed the problem in just those terms. What
rather concerned them was to analyze, with a view to
finding practical solutions for, a society that they all saw as
it really was: at only an initial stage of its unification,
disorganized, and above all sick. And if they posed the
problem in terms of a "society," rather than in terms of a
"nation," this is because they were all fully aware that
during their lifetimes the "nation" was more of a possibility
than an achieved reality. Such an awareness explains much
that has caused, and continues to cause, serious historical
confusions in Puerto Rico. For example, it explains the fact
that the great majority of Puerto Rican political leaders in
the nineteenth century were assimilationists early on and
autonomists later, with separatism only managing to attract
a few. But it also explains something even more important in
view of what happened after 1898, which is that
separatism has always nourished in its bosom two dissimilar
ideological tendencies: the Antillean independentism,
whose greatest exponent was Betances, and the pro-
American annexionism of men like Henna and Todd —
tendencies united rather by their common antagonism to
Spain than by any shared nationalist aspiration. In truth
(and for its relevance to the development of a Puerto Rican
national consciousness) the more advanced sector of the
autonomist movement obviously deserves more credit than

the annexionist sector of the separatist movement, which incidentally explains Cuban independentist José Martí's sympathetic and laudatory opinion of Puerto Rican autonomist Baldorioty de Castro.[27] But annexionism, which along with separatism and autonomism embodied one of the main tendencies of Puerto Rican liberalism, wasn't however intrinsically hostile to the autonomist cause as is proved by the example of José Celso Barbosa and the other "pure" autonomists who with him founded the annexionist *Partido Republicano* soon after the Americans took over the colony.

The case of Hostos, Hostos being who he was, provides the best example of the awareness to be found among the most representative writers of the period of how fragile was any sense of a Puerto Rican national consciousness. Hostos had been a separatist and independentist from 1869 on, at which time he gave up hope that Spain would grant the autonomy that until then he had believed in. Yet when he returned to the island almost thirty years later, it wasn't immediate independence that he campaigned for. The reason for this wasn't that he never believed the United States would grant Puerto Rico independence, but that the reality he faced on his return led him to the conclusion that "the individual and social weaknesses everywhere visible seem to have made our people incapable of helping themselves." What Hostos then petitioned the United States for was for the latter to grant Puerto Rico disinterested help for a twenty-year period, so as to allow the Puerto Rican people — that "little nation," as he once called them in a moment of sorrowful tenderness — the opportunity to prepare themselves for a responsible choice of their definitive political status. To further this ambition he even shelved his own ideological principles, founding the League of Patriots as a political instrument through which he tried (but failed) to unite autonomists, independentists, and annexionists for the good of the country as a whole.

Neither Hostos nor any other Puerto Rican intellectual of his day was indifferent to what is today called the problem of national identity. But the truth is, this identity featured for those intellectuals less as an immediate issue than as a project for the future. It was an identity they saw *prefigured* in themselves, a small educated minority within a larger society, which was submerged in an obscurantism imposed by Spanish colonial rule. Their struggle, reformist for some and revolu-tionary for others, was always directed by their faith in progress, and the fact that they saw this progress as coming under the aegis of the social class to which they themselves belonged was perfectly natural, since it was the role of the creole bourgeoisie, by historical imperative, to take the lead in the fulfilment of this particular stage of the development of Puerto Rican society. This they all knew (although they couldn't quite express themselves in those terms) so that what in fact characterized their struggle was tenacity rather than desperation.

Desperation came later, caused, as I have already pointed out, by what the transference of colonial suzerainty from Spain to the United States meant for the most important sector of the creole ruling class. There isn't space in this brief exposition to give a detailed account of this process, but I don't think we are falsifying historical truth if we say that what happened was essentially the margination and expropriation of that same sector by American capitalism in its phase of imperialist expansion. Now, we all know that every ruling class identifies itself with the nation as a whole, seeing in its own internal and external enemies the enemies of the whole nation, and in its own crisis the nation's crisis. The crisis that the development of dependent capitalism, imposed by the American regime, inflicted on the Puerto Rican ruling class has had many diverse consequences and manifestations, one of which — and it is a consequence that particularly concerns us here — has to do with national identity, both as a concept and as a problem.

Let us start from a premise that I believe to be an evident truth, which is that the different social classes into which Puerto Rican society, like all class-based societies, has been divided, have never conceived or defined the issue of national identity in quite the same terms. Lenin's well-known thesis postulating "two cultures" at the heart of any class society, a culture of the oppressed and a culture of the oppressors, has only recently begun to be applied with any degree of scientific rigor to the case of Puerto Rico. But in future one can, and indeed should, insist that in Puerto Rico, as in any other country, these "two cultures" aren't sealed off from one another but intercommunicate, with the culture of the dominating class influencing that of the dominated class and vice-versa. The effects of this intercommunication have created the illusion, for certain superficial observers, of a cultural homogeneity that strictly speaking *can't* exist in a society divided into classes, and still less so when this division includes a strong racial component.

The culture of the oppressed in Puerto Rico has three recognizable sources or historical ingredients: first, cultural survivals of the indigenous world, subjugated and promptly wiped out by the Spanish invaders; and second and third, the still living contributions of the once-enslaved black population, and of the essentially white peasantry. As for the indigenous element, before one gives a confident opinion on how important it has in fact been — and that it *was* important isn't seriously in doubt — perhaps one should wait for the publication of studies in depth, examining the cultural interchanges that surely must have taken place in the first years of colonization between aborigines, Europeans, and transplanted Africans. However, as far as the African roots of Puerto Rican popular culture are concerned, I am convinced that the basic racism of the Puerto Rican ruling class has done all it can, sometimes with brutal frankness and at other times with a subtlety worthy of a better cause, to sidestep, repress, or distort their importance. Isabelo Zenón Cruz has given ample proof of this in his *Narciso descubre su trasero*[29] and I have already alluded to some of the underlying causes of this attitude in my *Conversación* with Arcadio Díaz Quiñones (*op. cit.*, pp. 45–46).

But to return to the specific theme of this essay, I must affirm that it will be obvious for anyone familiar with the literature produced by the Puerto Rican ruling class, that the idea of national identity this literature expresses (if and when it *does* express it) usually leaves out, or underrates to a degree that is virtually equivalent to an omission, the black ingredient in our national identity. And it does so, not by accident or moral perversity, but for historical reasons that are readily explained. It is in no way fortuitous that the most representative writers of the twentieth-century creole bourgeoisie have done something their predecessors never did in the nineteenth century, which is to see the basically white peasantry — in other words, the *jíbaro* — as the quintessential incarnation of the "national soul." This appropriation by the culture of the oppressors — of the *local* oppressors, as opposed to those oppressors from abroad that a colonial society also has to suffer — of one of the two roots of the culture of the oppressed, privileging it above the other (black and mulatto) root, has for fifty years increasingly characterized most of what the Puerto Rican élite has written this century, from the very first stage of our literature after the Americans arrived onward.

That first stage obviously began immediately after the change of colonial regimes in 1898 and its most representative ideologues were José de Diego and Rosendo Matienzo Cintrón. Neither of these two men cultivated what only later came to be called *jibarismo literario* or the literary cult of the *jíbaro*, but both wrote works — albeit dissimilar and even contradictory in certain fundamental respects, as we shall soon see — that reveal preoccupations and attitudes prefiguring and explaining the final development in our "national" literature of the *jíbaro* theme. José de Diego's reaction to the change of regime is well known: he exalted Spanish cultural values as against those of the new metropolis — to the degree that he understood the latter, needless to say.[30] For De Diego, Puerto Rican identity was essentially Spanish, white, and Catholic, in other words a *creole* identity and without any traces of the African as a determining factor. The values of this identity were essentially those of a "Latin" culture transplanted to America. What all this expressed was a defensive attitude bent on preserving the social, economic, political, and cultural hegemony of the creole landowners and professionals, amongst whose ranks the changes that were beginning to take place in Puerto Rican society had aroused acute feelings of uncertainty and insecurity.

The contradiction that has sometimes been noted between De Diego's independentism and his professional status as an attorney for American sugar corporations was in fact merely one example of the overall contradiction inherent in the creole bourgeoisie's two main aspirations throughout this century: to create a State capable of perpetuating their own local hegemony and to obtain free access to the rich American markets. If the nationalist exegetes of De Diego would only remember that the independence their hero generally espoused was in fact an independence under American protection, no one would then be startled by De Diego's apparent "double personality" as politician and corporation lawyer. And everyone would then also easily realize why De Diego was one of the fiercest adversaries of the Puerto Rican labor movement in those same years. Without a doubt, that movement constituted the most powerful local challenge to the creole bourgeoisie's aspirations to hegemony and saw itself as having profited from the social legislation that the American unions had achieved under the conditions of an advanced capitalism. In fact, Puerto Rico at that time was inexorably moving toward integration into "a world community," but in a sense that can have given little joy to the conservative statesman De Diego.

In Matienzo Cintrón's case, we can note a significant difference. Matienzo, more advanced ideologically than De Diego as the spokesman for a petite bourgeoisie that didn't see itself as specially benefiting from the autonomist bargain with Spain (in fact Matienzo continued to be anti-autonomist even under the American regime), had a conception of Puerto Rican identity quite without the nostalgia for the past that characterized De Diego's conception of that identity. What greatly preoccupied Matienzo was the way landowners were being expropriated at the hands of absentee American capital; hence his emphasis on the preservation of agrarian ownership and on the creation of banks and businesses based on the accumulation of Puerto Rican funds. Matienzo's insistence on the importance of land was destined, in the following decades, to become the ideological foundation, often idealized to the point of mythification, of the tellurism that would dominate Puerto Rican literature from Luis Lloréns Torres and Miguel Meléndez Muñoz, to Enrique A. Laguerre, Emilio S. Belaval, Manuel Méndez Ballester, and Abelardo Díaz Alfaro. Nonetheless, Matienzo recognized that certain changes introduced by the new regime were in fact irreversible: "Just as we can't cease to be Puerto Rico however much time goes by, so nothing in the world can transform us into the Puerto Rico we once were." And he not only recognized the irrevocability of the changes to date, but also welcomed with enthusiasm those aspects of change that he considered positive: "To infuse our race with Yankee spirit, or in other words, to ballast the vessel of our imagination and stoke the almost extinct furnace of our energy with some shovelfuls of foreign coal, is a benefit that this foreign invasion has brought to our shores. Let us therefore profit by the occasion and let us bless it."

Anyone who sees in these remarks any tendency to a new assimilationism would however be in error, given what Matienzo says next: "But we will never tolerate our undoing or annihilation. Let us be as indispensable in the creation, not merely of Puerto Rico, but of the [Latin] American world as a whole, as is hydrogen in the creation of water. We must count on it or else perish of thirst."[32] Matienzo's independentism and Hispanoamericanism, the second incarnated in the character "Pancho Ibero" he invented, were based, as in the case of his contemporary Nemesio Canales, on a profound belief in democracy: "What would it matter should our flag emerge triumphant on the battlefield, as did the flags of Bolivar, San Martín, or Martí, were we to establish our republic, not so much upon a liberal constitution, as upon the caprices of cruel, immoderate Caesars?" (*op. cit.*, p. 171). Hence his agreement with Hostos on the need to educate the public for a certain period, until they became capable of responsibly deciding their own destiny: "First we shall identify our vices. Then, these eradicated, we shall identify our virtues and thereon base the right to demand our liberty. . . . The job will be one of educating the people to know how to benefit from their liberty, and for this, time is needed. I suggested thirty years, but without any dogmatic intention whatsoever." (*ibid.*)

What from another point of view could be called a lack of faith or confidence in the Puerto Rican people, was for these men merely an acute awareness of the lamentable state of civic unpreparedness to which Spanish colonialism had reduced Puerto Rico. And there is something else, too, we must keep in mind if we wish to understand the true nature of Puerto Rican liberal independentism in the first years of this century: all those men were keenly aware of the spectacle offered by the majority of Latin-American nations that had won their independence in the preceding century, but had since suffered alternating bouts of anarchy and dictatorship utterly destructive of real progress. They saw the causes of this collective misfortune in the hateful Spanish legacy of backwardness and despotism, as Martí and many other Hispanoamerican revolutionaries and reformers had done earlier. It was in Matienzo and Canales that the nineteenth-century progressive tradition of the Puerto Rican bourgeois intelligentsia found its worthy successors; like their forebears, they continued to see the definitive establishment of nationhood as a project for the future, and they continued to see themselves as its architects and custodians.

The conservatism and liberalism that are mutually exclusive in De Diego and Matienzo reappear two decades later in contradictory co-existence in the work of Antonio S. Pedreira. The oft-commented-on ideological ambiguity of Pedreira's *Insularismo* is, in the final analysis, one more sign of the creole bourgeoisie's incapacity to resolve *as a class* the contradictions inherent in its two historical aspirations this century: hegemony at home and participation in the dazzling affluence of American capitalism abroad. *Insularismo* was intended to assume a place in the critical nonconformist tradition of nineteenth-century Puerto Rican literature and to bring that tradition up to date. But Pedreira's analysis of our collective deficiencies is based on his essentially conservative viewpoint, which stands in stark contrast to the basically progressive point of view of an Alejandro Tapia, as we have already noted. Earlier we said that the contrast may be seen in the two writers' divergent opinions on the role of women in society, but it can also be noticed, once we situate ourselves within the appropriate context of each period, in what each has to say on the racial question. Whereas Tapia in 1882 saw slavery as the principal cause of Puerto Rico's backwardness and stagnation, Pedreira fifty years later, in 1934, saw in the country's blacks and mulattos, respectively, the origins of the passivity and lack of definition that in his view afflicted the national character.

It is certainly not by chance that women, blacks, and mulattos have been the main beneficiaries of the social and economic transformations that have occurred in Puerto Rico as a result of the development of dependent capitalism under the American regime. The relative progress — "relative" as dependent and colonial, but real and objective none the less — that women, blacks, and mestizos have enjoyed in Puerto Rico could only have been a negative and irritating factor for the traditional bourgeoisie, with their aspirations to local hegemony. At the same time, it was a factor inseparable from the process of Puerto Rican participation in the American economy. The ambiguity inherent in all Pedreira's social thought — the never resolved tension between his attachment to roots that were sickly or moribund, and his often acute perception of new realities — is revealed, to cite only one example, in the fact that the racist ideologue of *Insularismo* was also the enthusiastic biographer of José Celso Barbosa, the talented mulatto, who, as a radical autonomist under the Spanish and a convinced annexionist under the Americans, managed to set his mark upon a whole epoch of Puerto Rican politics.[33]

The marked subjectivism that dominates many of Pedreira's analyses meets its negative corollary, albeit only in a partial and limited manner, in the work of the other important essayist of the Generation of the 1930s, Tomás Blanco. Now, it is a well-known fact that *Prontuario histórico de Puerto Rico* (Historical Handbook to Puerto Rico) was motivated, at least in part, by Blanco's hostile reactions to many of Pedreira's arguments in *Insularismo*.

What Blanco set out to do in *Prontuario histórico de Puerto Rico* was to correct Pedreira's subjectivism by providing an objective foundation for his own personal interpretation of Puerto Rican historical reality. To the extent that he succeeded, the *Prontuario* is a more rational and lucid book, and more "scientific," than *Insularismo*, even though it too shows some of the limitations inherent in the vision of a social class in historical decline. Still, Blanco's effort to be objective led him to correct, to a considerable extent some of Pedreira's more reactionary positions, such as the racism I mentioned earlier. And another important element to Blanco's ideological credit is that he was basically immune to the sentimental Hispanophilia that characterized several of the other prominent members of his generation.

And now, having reached this point we must inevitably pause for a moment at the singular and surprising figure of Luis Palés Matos. The path followed by this great poet from "Pueblo negro" to "Mulata Antilla," or rather, the progressive refinement, without precedent in Puerto Rican literature, of a conception of the national genetics, is a path of unique and definitive discovery into the Afro-Antillean roots of our identity as a people. The unprecedented virulence of the attacks on Palés's theme of *negrismo* (negritude) voiced by many of the then outstanding representatives of *criollismo* and literary "avant-gardism" — J. I. de Diego Padró, José Antonio Dávila, Graciany Miranda Archilla, and others — is yet one further example of how the Puerto Rican cultural élite was increasingly reluctant to face the problem of national identity from an unprejudiced and realistic perspective. The historical deterioration of the social class from which this élite derived its values prevented it from recognizing the root-and-branch significance of Palés's message: either Puerto Ricans see themselves as they really are, realizing that they share their destiny in common with *all* the Antillean peoples, or they will have to forfeit their self-respect and everyone else's respect as well. When the most authoritative spokesmen for this élite weren't referring to Palés as a woolly-minded "exoticist," or as a particularly acerbic critic of creole mediocrity, they limited themselves to the examination and celebration of his undeniable qualities as a formal innovator. Of course, the many studies that concentrate on these aspects of Palés's work aren't to be sneered at, but the richness and ideological scope of this work certainly require a more comprehensive and inclusive treatment at some future date.[34]

The fact that Palés never formed a "school" of Puerto Rican poetry, if one puts aside several well-intentioned but superficial imitators, doesn't mean that his contribution to the awareness of national identity vanished into thin air. In the fiction and theater of the following generations (though less so in the poetry), one notices the influence of this new sense of national identity. Novels like *Usmail* by Pedro Juan Soto and *Una gota de tiempo* by César Andreu Iglesias, and *Vejigantes* and other plays by Francisco Arrivi, pose the problem of national identity in terms of a racial identity, with the mulatto conceived as the defining synthesis of what is truly "Puerto Rican." So, too, the vigorous *Cinco cuentos negros* by Carmelo Rodríguez Torres and the ongoing literary production of an exceptionally talented young writer like Edgardo Rodríguez Juliá, to mention only two examples, have begun a promising exploration in depth of the same subject-matter. However, we should be making a mistake if we did not recognize the survival of the old values in the work of as outstandingly important a writer as René Marqués. In the celebrated "return to the land" of *La Carreta*, in the exacerbated anti-feminism of "En la popa hay un cuerpo reclinado" and of other stories and plays, in the longing for an idealization of a patriarchal agrarian society in *La víspera del hombre,* and in the ahistorical subjectivism of "El puertorriqueño dócil" and *La mirada,* René Marqués's varied and prolific writings constitute a moving search for a "lost world," that expressions of militant nostalgia will never be sufficient to retrieve.

Be all that as it may (and the immediate future will soon prove us right or wrong), it would seem at last as though the long transforming parenthesis first opened by the *Real Cédula de Gracias* of 1815 is now finally about to close.

(1978)

NOTES

1. *Literatura y sociedad en Puerto Rico.* México, Fondo de Cultura Económica (Colección Tierra Firme), 1976, p. 95.

2. A satirical word meaning literally "little whites," but implying a sense of racial and social superiority. [Trans.]

3. Numerous official documents of the period, quoted by various Puerto Rican historians, testify to the terror stirred up in government circles by the possibility of a "Haitian contagion" among blacks and mulattos on the island. This consciousness of the danger represented by slave unrest last century provides the historical setting for a recent novel by the Puerto Rican writer Edgardo Rodríguez Juliá, *La renuncia del héroe Baltasar* (Editorial Antillana, Río Piedras, 1974).

4. The weakest part of this group, that had suffered exactions both from the regime itself and from the Spanish merchants, expressed their discontent on various occasions, the most important of these being the separatist rising at Lares in 1868.

5. The case of Gregorio Medina is illustrative in this respect. Medina, a sugar cane proprietor in Santo Domingo,

emigrated to Puerto Rico in the first years of the century. He settled in Ponce and grew to be the richest man in the area and one of the fourteen well-to-do voters on the island.

6. "Ruling," above all, in a social and, more specifically, cultural sense. There is little doubt that throughout this period, and, generally speaking, throughout the century as a whole, it was the representatives of the Spanish colonial regime on the island who exercised both economic and political power.

7. It doesn't escape my attention that this characterization of the blacks and mulattos in Puerto Rico as "the cement of nationality" will disconcert many readers. However it is a certain and well-documented fact that the white population, throughout the first century of Puerto Rican society, was profoundly unstable, being characterized by a propensity to abandon the island and establish itself in other richer colonies whenever the opportunity offered itself. In 1534 Governor Francisco Manuel de Lando declared: "Many colonists, maddened by the news from Peru, have sailed away in secret from remote harbors on our coasts. Of the colonists who remain, even those who have put down the strongest roots pray daily, 'May God carry me off to Peru!' Night and day I go about spying to see that no one gets away and I am by no means certain that I shall be able to keep people at home." Later, in begging for "favors and privileges for so noble an island," he draws attention to how Puerto Rico "was so depopulated that one hardly ever sees a Spanish face but only negroes." In such conditions, how can one not believe that black slaves and their immediate descendants, prevented from emigrating or returning to Africa, were the first to realize that they *had* to adapt themselves for good to the Puerto Rican milieu and so feel the insular territory as their only possible fatherland?

8. Dark in color, clear in brow,/ A languid, proud and penetrating gaze,/ Beard black and pale complexion,/ A lean countenance and well-proportioned nose.

Of medium height and regulated pace;/ The soul tremulous with dreams,/ A wit at once keen and free and proud,/ Restless in thought and with an ardent mind;

Humane, affable, fair, generous,/ Always changeable in love,/ Eager in pursuit of glory or of pleasure,

Unsurpassable in love of country./ Here, you may be sure, is a true sketch/ From which to copy [a good likeness] of the Puerto Rican!

9. The term "creole bourgeoisie," even when it is qualified by the adjectives "new" and "incipient," has been criticized by students of Puerto Rican social history, who would prefer the term "landowning class" since they believe such a term, unlike "creole bourgeoisie," doesn't imply capitalist development in Puerto Rico. In a strict sense they may be right. However, I have used the term "creole bourgeoisie" in a broader sense to refer to a class that owned the important means of production in the nineteenth century.

10. *Mea culpa*: in an earlier stage of my examination of Puerto Rican literary history I myself referred to *El gíbaro* as the "corner-stone" of the national literature (*Literatura y sociedad*, p. 193).

11. There is certainly no lack of very explicit references, in the bibliography on eighteenth and nineteenth-century Puerto Rico, to the abysmal differences between "those at the top" and "those at the bottom" in Puerto Rican society. Here I only wish to quote a passage from a little-known text *El último alcalde español en las Américas*, by Rafael Martínez Alvarez (the biography of D. Fermín Martínez y Villamil, who was the mayor of San Juan at the time of the American invasion in 1898, published in Mexico, Imp. Manuel

León Sánchez, in 1947). The author here describes a social gathering in a Puerto Rican *hacienda* in the second half of the nineteenth century:

> Once the daily tasks are over, the social gathering of dinner guests takes place in don Pablo's house. The guests, having enjoyed a sumptuous meal, now chat, laugh, tell funny stories, gossip, and argue. Meanwhile, on the beaten earth in front of a humble store, by the side of a nearby road, a social gathering of peons, sweaty and tired, stifle their hunger by gorging fritters, fried codfish, and coconut candies. Here are two totally different ethnic groups, the white group indoors and the black group squatting by the side of the road. The first group comfortable in armchairs and rocking-chairs, the second crouched on their heels as though about to make a spring like caged beasts. Indoors, cigars and cigarettes. By the roadside, pies and wads of tobacco. Inside, champagne, beer, and wines. Outside, sugarcane juice, *maví*, and rum. In both places the cesation [sic] from labor — but indoors with delight, outdoors with sullen resignation. . . . In the discussion "upstairs" the guests discussed assorted topics, amongst which the most burning ones touch on the mysterious jungle of historical events. . . . "Downstairs," nothing lucid emerged in the discussion from the thicket of negroid contortions, obfuscated by the inextricable tangles of kinky, curly hair.

The blatant racism of the author, himself a Puerto Rican from "upstairs," only confirms the exactness of his vision of a society that was as divided economically as it was racially.

12. The letter was intended to launch a subscription on behalf of Tapia's widow and orphan children, left destitute by the writer's death.

13. The book was first published in 1927 in the newspaper *La Democracia*, edited by Antonio R. Barceló. It has since been published in three further editions (1928, 1946 and 1967).

14. Alejandro Tapia y Rivera, *Mis memorias*, San Juan, Editorial Coquí, 1967, p. 89.

15. And can anyone say with certainty that Zeno and Del Valle didn't know the book because it hadn't yet been published? There is an interesting fact which should at least suggest caution in this respect. The allusion to the *Aguinaldo puertorriqueño* of 1843 as "the first infant cry of the Puerto Rican muse" is generally attributed to Salvador Brau, who certainly used the metaphor in his 1884 prologue to the second edition of Manuel Alonso's *El gíbaro*. But Tapia in *Mis memorias*, referring to the *Album Puertorriqueño* of 1844 and to the *Cancionero de Borinquen* of 1846, had already written: "There are books which have more than mere literary importance for us, since they are in fact the first essays or infant cries of the Puerto Rican muse. . . ." (*Mis memorias,* ed. *cit.,* p. 122). Merely a coincidence, or had Tapia read these words to some of his writer friends, in whole or in part, from his manuscript of *Mis memorias*? If Brau was one of their number and committed the metaphor to heart, later repeating it without remembering its origin, then why couldn't Zeno and Del Valle also have known the text before its publication? It should be remembered that literary discussion groups, or *tertulias*, were very much in vogue throughout this period.

16. Arcadio Díaz Quiñones, *Conversación con José Luis González*, San Juan, Ediciones Huracán, 1976, pp. 66–67.

17. This chapter was originally read as a paper at the "Coloquio sobre Identidad Caribeña: Puerto Rico y Haití" held at Princeton University, April 10–12, 1978. [Trans.]

18. Antonio S. Pedreira, *Insularismo*, Madrid, Tipografía Artística, 1934, p. 60.

19. Francisco Manrique Cabrera, *Historia de la literatura puertorriqueña,* Río Piedras, Editorial Cultural, 1973, p. 91.

20. *Literatura y sociedad en Puerto Rico,* p. 107.

21. This was a modernizing dynamism that, in Puerto Rico as in any other country submitted to a colonial regime, implied both a certain degree of progress in certain aspects and stages of the colonizing process, and also serious material and cultural deformities, known and well documented in our own times.

22. *Insularismo,* ed. cit., pp. 64–65. The true nature of Tapia's cosmopolitanism can be seen in the following passage from *Mis memorias:* "As it wasn't possible for me to become an enlightener or benefactor of the human race, I decided that the poor inhabitants of my own country, both present and future, also belonged to humanity, were part of it and had the right to be so. . . . My fortune, my situation and my feelings led me to care deeply, intensely, for the well-being of this handful of earth, which is also part of the world. . . . Everything is lacking in this tiny corner of the world, and, above all, men of good will of whom there aren't anything like enough to serve her well. Compared with other lands, this island is almost like an ingénue, in its slow and hesitating steps towards enlightenment and well-being. Three centuries of lethargy and ignorance, of unconscious but harmful egotism, could hardly have produced any other results. May Puerto Rico be the world for those who love her!" (*Mis memorias,* ed. cit., p. 66).

23. It should be remembered, because it is relevant to the argument, that Zeno began his literary career writing "cosmopolitan" stories: *Rosa de mármol* (1889) and *Piccola* (1890), set respectively in Pisa and Milan.

24. Hostos appears to refer here to the Spanish policy of transplanting people from unprotected to protected areas (e.g. from rural to urban areas) in times of danger. [Trans.]

25. Eugenio María de Hostos, "El próposito político de la Liga de Patriotas," in *Madre Isla, Obras Completas*, vol. V, La Habana, 1939, pp. 26–27.

26. Salvador Brau, *Disquisiciones sociológicas y otros ensayos*, Ediciones del Instituto de Literatura, Universidad de Puerto Rico, 1956, pp. 160–61.

27. "For him autonomy wasn't merely an exchange of gifts with some friendly general or other, who would hang tomorrow someone he played chess with today, but instead the true defense, by way of jail, misery and exile, of the liberties Baldorioty always served — for liberty was never as far advanced in Puerto Rico as Baldorioty's aspirations for it. Autonomy was for Baldorioty — a Creole both direct and practical — the way of uniting the irreducible forces of his country, in accordance with its geography and history, as indeed they must be united so as to establish a happier form of government, in peace and order, the day when autonomy is discovered to be insufficient (as it would be found the very day it was granted!) or else unobtainable. . . . The three brother peoples, the three islands [of Cuba, Puerto Rico, and Santo Domingo] who must either choose joint salvation or joint perdition, have done well to crown with flowers . . . the good, the pure, the shrewd, the rebellious, the founder, the American, Ramón Baldorioty de Castro." (José Martí, "Las Antillas y Baldorioty de Castro" in *Obras Completas*, vol 4, La Habana, Editorial Nacional de Cuba, pp. 409–410). On another occasion Martí referred to Baldorioty's political behavior as "the slow readying of a character for revolutionary action." ("'¡Vengo a darte patria!,' Puerto Rico y Cuba" in *Obras Completas, ed. cit.*, vol 2, p. 259.)

28. The local *ruling* class that, by virtue of the colonial statute in force in the country, is partly subordinated and partly allied to the *dominant* class, consisting of the monopolist bourgeoisie and the American political bureaucracy.

29. A punning title: either "Narciso Discovers his Backside," or "Narciso Uncovers his Backside." [Trans.]

30. De Diego, as is well known, was much better versed in the Latin cultures of Europe than in Anglo-Saxon culture. His knowledge of American culture, a culture that Martí and other Hispanoamericans of his time knew so well, was doubtless very limited. This certainly prevented him from discerning the deepest implications of the changes that the forced coexistence of two cultural traditions in Puerto Rico, the American and the Spanish, then began to exert upon the Puerto Rican mentality.

31. We refer to hegemony at a *local* level, as we have already indicated in note 28.

32. Rosendo Matienzo Cintrón, "Violada el alma jurídica" in Luis M. Díaz Soler, *Rosendo Matienzo Cintrón, recopilación de su obra escrita*, tomo II, Ediciones del Instituto de Literatura Puertorriqueña, Universidad de Puerto Rico, 1960, pp. 194–195.

33. It is however revealing that in this biography of Barbosa, Pedreira praises the participation of one of Barbosa's ancestors in the putting-down of a slave rebellion.

34. Like that which the critic Arcadio Díaz Quiñones has been applying to Palés's work, to judge by his recent essays. No less worthy of notice is Margot Arce de Vásquez's sensible judgment, in her prologue to the *Poesia completa y prosa selecta* of Palés (Biblioteca Ayacucho, núm. 32, Caracas, 1978): "[Palés] called attention to Antillean unity so that we would recognize ourselves as Antilleans and seek solidarity between our peoples (as may clearly be seen in the second version of the poem *Mulata-antilla*, 1949). Black blood and black culture are constituent elements of this unity and have been, are, and will remain, a determining factor in the destiny and politico-economic liberation of these islands. . . . If these [Afro-Antillean] poems are read as they should be read, it will become manifest that they constitute

a testimony to Palés's commitment to his people, and of his political conscience as an anti-imperialist and as a pro-Antillean."

"Plebeyism" and Art in Today's Puerto Rico

José Ortega y Gasset is a thinker with whom I have fundamental differences, but it was nonetheless Ortega, writing about one of the splendid painters of his native land,* who rightly pointed to "a very strange phenomenon" in Spanish history, in fact so strange that Ortega claimed it was to be found "in no other country." One must of course assume that the other countries our philosopher from Madrid had in mind were other *European* countries, his well-known Eurocentrism invariably excluding from his purview the cultural realities of Africa and Asia. And as far as our own continent is concerned, all that interested him there, and even then only tangentially, were the two countries whose cultural Europeanization made them major exceptions within the context of the Americas: Argentina and the United States. Still, the fact is Ortega wasn't wrong when he called the phenomenon in question "very strange" and even when we examine it from a universalist perspective we are compelled to recognize its singularity.

To describe this phenomenon Ortega began by calling it "plebeyism," only to insist immediately that he meant something quite different from the "popularism" that traditional criticism has always attributed to Goya's painting and that, as Ortega himself pointed out, has proved to be "one of the deepest veins in continental [i.e. European] painting from the last third of the sixteenth century on. . . . From the shock of its influence sprung no less a painter than Velásquez." So that "to paint scenes of popular

---

*José Ortega y Gasset, *Goya*, El Arquero, Ediciones de la *Revista de Occidente*, Madrid, 1966.

life [i.e. "popularism"] was in no way distinctive in 1775."
Well now, "distinctive" in the highest degree — that is to
say, possessing a character exceptional for its originality —
is just how we should describe Goya's art so that it isn't so
much traditional "popularism" that describes it as
"plebeyism," a concept of which Ortega goes on to explain
the historical determinants :

> One can hardly exaggerate the degree to which the
> Spanish aristocracy decayed in the course of the second
> half of the seventeenth century. . . . By then it had lost
> all of its creative force. Not only did it show itself
> incompetent in politics, administration, and art, but
> also in the renovation, or even graceful preservation, of
> the forms of everyday life. In short, it ceased to
> exercise the principal function of an aristocracy, which
> is to set an example. A result of all this was that the
> people felt themselves unprotected and abandoned, and
> without any models, modalities, or disciplines handed
> down from above. Our common people then again
> demonstrated that strange power they have to *fare da
> se*, to live by themselves and for themselves and so
> derive nourishment from their own vitality and their
> own inspiration. I call this power "strange" because,
> taken all in all, it was very much less often found in
> nations than might be supposed. From 1670 on, the
> Spanish "plebs" began to live turned in upon
> themselves. Instead of searching outside for their forms
> of life, they began little by little to refine and stylize
> the forms that were traditionally theirs (which didn't
> prevent them from making use of this or that element
> borrowed from the nobility, but only after having
> remodelled it to suit themselves). From this
> spontaneous, diffuse and quotidian labor emerged that
> repertory of postures and gestures that has been typical

of the Spanish people for the past two centuries. This repertory has a character that makes it into something I believe to be unique: though it consists, as in all popular cultures, of movements and attitudes that are spontaneous, yet those movements and attitudes have become *stylized*. Our people recreated for themselves a sort of second nature that was informed by qualities that were basically aesthetic. And that repertory of lines and rhythms, employed in every waking moment, constituted a vocabulary, a precious raw material, from which emerged the popular arts. What these in fact represented, then, was a second deliberated stylization, that imposed itself on the first by constant movement, gesticulation, and conversation.

Historical realities in Spain in the second half of the seventeenth century, and in Puerto Rico in the second half of the twentieth, are no doubt very different, but it is nevertheless remarkable how the situations in both countries are somewhat analogous. Only a year or so ago, in an exchange of letters with Arcadio Díaz Quiñones I argued that the leading social class in Puerto Rico had begun to lose the economic strength necessary for its cultural supremacy when American monopoly capitalism irrupted into Puerto Rico after 1898 — and when I say "irrupted" I am thinking of the military and political aspects of the American invasion, since the economic penetration had begun much earlier. This new colonization steadily undermined the creole bourgeoisie's economic supremacy (exercised at the expense of the majority of the population, though not of the Spanish residents favored by the Spanish regime before 1898, or of the absentee American landlords favored thereafter) and also mediatized its political conduct — both to such a degree that this creole bourgeoisie found itself unable to mount a successful rebellion against a pernicious and menacing dependency and so had to go on the defensive and continue its resistance at the level of culture.

Whatever that resistance achieved — and it would be quite unfair to utterly dismiss it — what can't be denied is that it could not halt the deterioration of the creole ruling class at the hands of an imperial power now entering its final phase of economic, political, and cultural expansionism. The cultural values defended by that class were in a strict sense class values, but it is important to point out that where class values are also the values of a *national class*, which is to say the values of the ruling class of a society at a specific historical moment, then they are also national values to the degree that they have furthered national formation, since they are values that the nation as a whole has come to recognize. In the specific case of Puerto Rico, this process of national development, even if it hadn't got beyond its initial stages in 1898, had already advanced sufficiently for the creole bourgeoisie, incipient though it may have been, to see itself as leader and guardian of what was already coming to be seen as the national destiny. In this sense its cultural class-values had no rival in sight as the expression of the values of the nation as a whole.

The values of a single class cease to be national values only to the degree that that class ceases to play a leading role in society, even though it continues to exercise political and economic hegemony. That is precisely what began to happen to the Spanish aristocracy in the second half of the seventeenth century, with the result, as Ortega rightly points out, that that aristocracy was no longer capable of "setting an example." For this reason the Spanish people found themselves "unprotected and abandoned," "without models . . . handed down from above," and choosing to "live by themselves and for themselves, and so derive nourishment from their own vitality and their own inspiration." I should mention in fairness that this analogy between the Spanish

aristocracy's predicament then, and the Puerto Rican
bourgeoisie's predicament now, involves an important
difference — that the decadence of the former was self-
imposed, whereas the way the latter's destiny was
frustrated was the result of outside influences. This
difference is of some importance and needs further analysis
in some other context, but what matters here is to examine
the cultural consequences in both situations, since it is in
those consequences that the analogy resides. In our own creole
bourgeoisie today one in fact observes an incapacity "to set an
example" very similar to that which Ortega points to in the
Spanish aristocracy of three centuries ago; similarly, one
perceives in our own popular masses the same sense of being
"unprotected and abandoned," that forces them "to live by
and for themselves" and so to acquire in their daily lives and
through spontaneous creativity what Ortega calls "a sort of
second nature . . . informed by qualities that were basically
aesthetic." From that nature, which represents "a second
deliberated stylization that imposed itself on the first by
constant movement, gesticulation, and conversation," derive
the popular arts. Of these, there were two in particular that
were created by the Spanish people in the course of the
eighteenth century, as "a large part of the overwhelmingly
'plebeyist' current that almost completely inundated
Spanish society round about 1750": bull-fighting and the
theatre.

Let us now translate this phenomenon into terms of Puerto
Rico today by citing the people's passion for sport and their
"plebeyist" musical creativity, from *plena* to *salsa*. In both
the Spanish and Puerto Rican cases, the analogy allows a
sociological interpretation of a somewhat greater order of
complexity. In the Spanish case, a contest to the death
between man and bull was initially a sport reserved for the
aristocracy: men fought on horseback because it was
considered a heroic "sport" similar to war and hence suitable

only for gentlemen. When the people took the habit over they modified it in two essential respects. First, they fought on foot and second, they made the event a popular celebration. In other words, they plebeyized it.

But isn't this after all what has happened in Puerto Rico with the sports of baseball and basketball (still called *basquetbol*** in a majority of Spanish-speaking countries)? We aren't of course speaking here of pastimes inherited by the people from a national aristocracy, which strictly speaking has never existed among us. But baseball and basketball *did* in fact reach us from the equivalent of an "upper" or "superior" class, namely the class of foreigners turned overlords. From the beginning baseball and basketball were games with a populist appeal in the United States, but that doesn't invalidate the argument that they reached Puerto Rico wearing the halo of having originated in a society the Puerto Rican masses considered "superior," both because of its wealth and because it had defeated Spain. As anyone past his first prime can doubtless confirm, in Puerto Rico basketball was initially the sport of university students: affluent white boys, the sons of "good families," filled the courts (and weren't in fact the most-used courts in those early days built by the ultra-American, ultra-protestant Y.M.C.A.?). Moreover, anyone who has seen the game played both then and now can testify to the extent that many aspects of the sport have been plebeyized as a result of the people's widespread involvement, both as players and as spectators. This plebeyization is evident in the greater craftiness and daring of many of the plays, in the eagerness to cry foul, in the betting, and, above all, in the more or less disguised professionalism of the players, the same professionalism that in Spain, as Ortega reminds us, brought into being the *torero* — all of which marks basketball's

---

*The correct Spanish word is *baloncesto*. [Trans.]

democratizing spread from élite campuses to housing projects and ghettos.

In eighteenth-century Spain the popularity of the theatre occurred in a period otherwise marked by the extreme decadence of stagecraft as an art. "The plays of our old baroque theatre were staged and restaged a million times," Ortega tells us,

> but by now a variety of new theatrical forms had been introduced — one-act farces, the *jácara,* the *tonadilla* — some of plebeian origin and style, and others, such as the *zarzuela,* born at Court but increasingly marked by popular inspiration. These new genres lacked all literary value, indeed they never even claimed to possess any. . . . Beneath the archaic grime of our baroque theatre and side by side with the handful of imbecile authors who then cluttered our stage, an uninterrupted sequence of charming actresses and talented actors appeared after 1750, all of them, with very rare exceptions, of plebeian origins. The actresses were at one and the same time declaimers, singers, and dancers. . . . The actresses in particular must have been endowed with abundant personal charm and collectively constituted one of the most delightful flowerings of Spanish womanhood. No one had ever taught them the grace that gushed from them in torrents, carrying all before it. They transformed the theatre into what was virtually the mainspring of national life. Their popularity had no limits. Everyone knew, commented on, and discussed, not only the excellence of their acting on stage, but also the tiniest detail of their private lives.

Now, isn't all this in fact a description, *mutatis mutandis,* of a very obvious Puerto Rican passion today for show business, ranging from the trivial comedy programs on radio and television to the undulating scenic attractions of Iris Chacón? One difference between both situations, that one should mention to avoid misunderstandings, is that none of the handful of dramatists we can boast of today in Puerto Rico in fact deserves the hard Ortegian name of "imbecile." Quite the opposite, since in fact it is well known that the best of our contemporary dramatists can hold their own with any now writing in Spanish. I should also make it clear that I am fully conscious of the alienating effect of much of today's plebeian culture, as I am aware of (and in no way underestimate) the extent to which it has been commercialized. Exactly the same could be said of the bull--fighting and the sub-literary theatrical activity to which Ortega referred. But the main fact is indisputable: the Puerto Rican popular masses, increasingly orphaned by the absence of any "exemplarity" from a ruling class capable of supplying valid models for artistic creation, as in the recent and not-so-recent past, began some years ago to live "by themselves and for themselves" and so derive "nourishment from their own vitality and from their own inspiration." And in this context we should remember Ortega's distinction between popularism and plebeyism. There has always been popularism of superior quality in the best artistic productions of the Puerto Rican creole bourgeoisie, from Manuel Alonso's *El gíbaro* to the poetry of Luis Llórens Torres. However, what I am referring to now is something quite different. Popularism is the selection from above of forms from below that are not intended as models. Plebeyism is the creation of models from below and their imposition on what lies above. In Spanish painting, popularism is Velásquez and plebeyism is Goya; in Spanish literature, popularism is Galdós and plebeyism is the mature Valle Inclán. From these examples it should be obvious that it isn't so much a matter of making value judgments between individual artists, as of making historical and sociological distinctions between different forms of art.

The supreme examples, in my opinion, of the plebeyism now beginning to influence the arts in Puerto Rico are José Rosa in painting and Luis Rafael Sánchez in literature. Now, I am not a critic of art and it would be foolhardy of me to attempt a formal evaluation of Rosa's abundant and diverse work. And yet I have always been interested in it ever since I first got to know it many years ago, particularly in relation to all I have thought and said about plebeyism as an artistic current determined by a very unusual historical situation. What we have in Rosa, unless I am much mistaken, is the definitive and dazzling appearance in the Puerto Rican plastic arts of a way of living life that, in a radical and aggressive manner, reaches us *from below*. And, to avoid confusions, let me hurriedly explain that what is at issue is neither pictorial popularism nor pictorial primitivism. In popularism, as we all know, what is popularist is the *subject matter*, in the best of cases treated with sympathy but without any necessary or intrinsic identification between artist and subject. Popularist subjects have traditionally been the principal motif of the plastic arts in Puerto Rico, from Oller to the excellent engravers and serigraphers of recent years. But such a motif necessarily needs some *mediation* for it to become a valid creative expression of permanent value. In the last instance, that mediation has always been ideological, in the sense of the reverential acceptance of models handed down from above — or "from on high," as Ortega would prefer to say. The models we are discussing are of course cultural ones and that artists of humble origins should have accepted them in no way suggests that they have lacked talent or were disloyal to their class origins. What it *does* however imply is that these models continued to be valid, because no others appeared on the scene that were capable of supplanting them. The experts will tell us that this reverence for models "from above" has been in many cases more relative than absolute, and this, which is undoubtedly true, might oblige us to search out precedents for Rosa's work. As I am not an expert it isn't for me to attempt to identify these precedents, but even were I to identify them I should still feel obliged to suggest that José Rosa is the first Puerto Rican painter to have broken clearly with models "from on high" in a social and hence in an ideological sense. The popular in his work isn't merely in the subject matter or in the motifs displayed, but of the very essence, hence requiring no "mediation" to impose itself as a valid aesthetic creation in its own right.

On the other hand, nothing is further from primitivism than the work of an artist so consummately in control of the techniques of his art as is José Rosa. "Plebeyism" is just what this is, because only the creation of a life-style for the Puerto Rican masses, obliged as the Spanish had been when their ruling class was decadent to "live turned in upon themselves," to stop "searching outside for their forms of life," and to "refine and stylize the forms that were traditionally theirs" — only the creation of such a way of living, vitally plebeian and capable of the highest artistic flights, could have made possible an art like that of José Rosa. It is an art characterized by irreverence, by a mocking disdain for solemnity, by a suspicion of all sermonizing and speechifying, and by a habit of shunning all offers of salvation, either from abroad or from "on high," an art depending on its own moral and material resources, sly, impudent, and bold in its own crafty, anti-heroic way, an art through which the Puerto Rican masses, determined to survive "as best they may," find their own voice, despite their impatient or despairing critics.

I do not think that I am deceiving myself when I see in *La guaracha del macho Camacho*, the recent and very popular novel by Luis Rafael Sánchez, a second example of the way a plebeyist spirit has made its presence felt in the field of contemporary Puerto Rican artistic production. We are dealing here with an exceptionally cultivated artist, whose relations to literature aren't confined to creation but who is also a teacher and scholar; we must therefore assume that Sánchez is conscious of theoretical considerations, the practical application of which we can hardly analyze in the present context without running the risk of critical ingenuousness. For this reason we have to start with a recognition of aesthetic and ideological goals of some complexity, which were we to examine them without due interpretative caution, would lead us to neglect those literary qualities that are of prime importance. If as we said earlier the plebeyist element in José Rosa's work is of a piece with its artistic expression, in Luis Rafael Sánchez the plebeyism is both expressive recourse and intellectual presupposition. Here we are dealing with a writer, who, quite deliberately, has produced a text of ideological *rupture.* This is something that certain naively politicized critics of his work appear to have missed. All they manage to see in *La guaracha* is a denunciation of the socio-political situation in Puerto Rico, the novelty of which stems from the grotesco-popularist idiom employed throughout. But if this were *La guaracha*'s only originality, then we should have to consider it as no more than the epigone of Emilio Díaz Valcárcel's memorable *Figuraciones en el mes de marzo.* And this is evidently not the case.

However, if it is legitimate to see in *Figuraciones* the immediate and most obvious forerunner of *La guaracha,* this is because we find in *Figuraciones,* albeit only as one aspect of its complex structure, the defining characteristic of *La guaracha* in its entirety: the *assumption* of a reality, against which the author himself rebels from the depths of his being. We can take as an example the letters in *Figuraciones* that various Puerto Ricans write from the island to their compatriots living in Madrid. In the novel by Díaz Valcárcel these letters function as a sort of ideological counterpart to the protagonist's thoughts and vicissitudes. But by doing without a protagonist, or to put it more exactly, by making the protagonist the lyrics of a cheap popular song, Sánchez has turned his back on all ideological counterpointing to *assume* a reality that all we previous Puerto Rican writers had explored — and as often as not denounced — *through*, rather than *in*, our writing. This assumption of a social reality within the writing itself runs the risk of making less alert readers suspect that the author is indulging himself in a sort of gratuitous plebeyism. But nothing could be further from the truth, if I read Sánchez's intention correctly.

And since we are discussing intentions, let me hazard the opinion that *La guaracha del macho Camacho* is the first decisive effort in our literature to break (and hence my earlier allusion to "a text of ideological rupture") with a way of confronting reality that I would describe as exteriorist — which is to say, from a position above or outside that reality. But to write from *within* reality Luis Rafael Sánchez has had to assume that reality directly into his own person, with all its weight of plebeyist resoluteness and pathos, submissiveness and compassion, suspiciousness and sense of solidarity. In Sánchez's novel as in the paintings of José Rosa, the way the Puerto Rican masses see the world at last elbows its way into the limelight. Of course, this may not be the only way to create good literature in today's Puerto Rico, but it is undoubtedly one of the most effective and committed ways and one full of possibilities that our writers should learn to explore and exploit in future — providing, that is, they display the same lucidity and audacity already so impressively demonstrated by Luis Rafael Sánchez.

(1979)

The "Lamento Borincano":
A Sociological Interpretation

When I went to Mexico for the first time already more than thirty years ago, people there knew very little about Puerto Rico. However, there was one thing many Mexicans *did* know, which was that Puerto Rico was the home of Rafael Hernández. His "Lamento Borincano" then enjoyed and continues to enjoy today, in spite of the considerable time that has passed, a popularity equalled only by some of the songs of the best popular composers of the period such as Agustín Lara or Alberto Domínguez. But the fact remains that nowadays the "Lamento" continues to resurface on the radio programs of Mexico City and the provinces with an equal or greater frequency than it does in Puerto Rico itself, whereas even a "classic" of the genre like "Perfidia," which once took the world by storm in innumerable local versions, is a mere "nostalgia piece" in today's Mexico. (And if I may be permitted the autobiographical digression, how can I fail to remember that it was while dancing this bolero by Domínguez the summer of 1959 in a Prague nightclub that I began to court the young woman who a few months later agreed to join her life with mine?)

Personally, I believe that the durability — or perhaps even immortality, to use what is perhaps rather a startling word — of this song by our own Rafael Hernández has a sociological cause perhaps even more noteworthy than the artistic merits of the song itself. I stress *perhaps* because my extremely meagre musical knowledge disqualifies me from giving an opinion on this subject with any show of authority. Still, I remember having once read that Hernández himself initially felt so dissatisfied with his "Lamento" that he

85

was on the point of throwing it out, before he decided, no one knows why, to give it to the world. I cannot guarantee the truth of this story, but in any case, if the "Lamento Borincano" continues to exercise its spell over Latin-American sensibilities in spite of changes in musical taste, one reason, though there are others, is that, it expressed better than any other song a social reality that far from having become "past history," is still fully alive for most countries in that long-suffering continent. The tragedy of the Puerto Rican *jíbaro*, in the 1930s a helpless victim of poverty and spiritual malaise, is the tragedy of today's Salvadorian, Guatemalan, Bolivian, Paraguayan, or Ecuadorian peasant. (To set matters in their right perspective, we should add that in Puerto Rico this poverty has been dressed up in consumerist affluence, and this malaise in frivolity and unscrupulousness, but there is no Puerto Rican, however deluded and irresponsible, who does not feel them breathing down his neck.)

If I am not mistaken, the "Lamento" was Latin America's first "protest song" and I know of no other piece of music of the genre to which it belongs — a genre increasingly subject, I fear, to the claims of an industry run, like all industries, for profit — that can rival it in sustained popularity. Even today the Mexico where this native of Aguadilla spent his best years continues to remember him as "the little *jíbaro*," in homage to the song he wrote and to the country of his birth.

If the "Lamento" is in fact Latin America's first "protest song," then I should point out that there is an essential difference between it and most of the protest songs being written today. (I refer, of course, only to the lyrics, which is all I feel myself competent to give an opinion about without exposing myself to the charge of glaring ignorance.) The lyrics of the "Lamento," as we all know, narrate — *narrate* rather than *preach*, an important difference — a personal experience which only acquires a collective significance as it passes through the reader's — in this case, auditor's — consciousness, partly because this experience was a *typical* experience in a Puerto Rico then in the throes of an economic crisis, but above all, it seems to me, because the author refrains from making assertions about the causes or consequences of the situation his hero lives through and confines himself instead to a final question: "What will become of Borinquen, dear God, what will become of my children and my home?"

The question of course implied a commitment that, without forcing matters, we could term ideological, but the commitment was expressed at a human and individual level, which, merely by being human, grew to be social, so that Borinquen (the country, society in general) came to be identified with the more particular and intimate (the children and the home). There was no overt judgment in the song, but instead the reference to a reality that all Puerto Ricans could immediately recognize even if they hadn't all experienced it to the same degree. Nor did the lyrics voice an explicit demand for freedom. What they *did* voice was an accusation in the form of a "lament," which is the least aggressive, though by no means the least eloquent, of all forms of accusation. It is significant that a few years later the same Hernández composed the equally well-known and ever-popular "Preciosa," where the political protest is quite overt. In fact, it was so overt that the mean-spirited attempt to denature it (at whose instigation, I wonder?) by converting an easily identifiable "tyrant" into a vague "destiny" was promptly rejected by a public by then no longer willing to put up with such a shabby trick of substitution. "Preciosa" wasn't in fact composed in response to an economic crisis, as the "Lamento" had been, but instead, as now seems very obvious to me, in response to a crisis of political consciousness provoked by the nationalist movement and by the wave of repression unleashed against it by the colonial regime.

I find all of this interesting, because in today's Puerto Rico as elsewhere there is an on-going debate on how to create a "political art" capable of reaching the masses at whom it is consciously aimed. I believe that the history of Puerto Rican literature at both the "cultivated" and "popular" levels can offer us some useful lessons here. Forty years before Rafael Hernández wrote the "Lamento Borincano," Lola Rodríguez and Pachín Marín cultivated an explicitly political, revolutionary poetry, intended, they declared, to awaken and inspire the independence movement then actively opposing Spanish colonial rule. Lola, as is well known, tried to combine her poetic efforts with other forms of popular entertainment by writing new subversive lyrics (in the most honest and respectable sense of the word "subversive") for "La Borinqueña."* What now needs to be explained is why the poetry of Lola and Pachín never made an impression on the Puerto Rican masses as the "Lamento Borincano" and "Preciosa" were later to do.

One explanation may be that poetry is written to be read and cannot therefore reach a public that is illiterate, as were the great majority of Puerto Ricans in the last century. But this argument has never quite convinced me, since the popular masses in Argentina were also illiterate and yet made José Hernández's *Martín Fierro* very much their own by memorizing and transmitting it orally. Similarly, the Cuban masses took to their hearts much of the poetry of José Martí and in particular his *Versos sencillos*. The same Puerto Rican public, much more literate in the '40s of this century than at the end of the nineteenth century (though still without a taste for reading), took to heart the "cultivated" verses of Lloréns Torres and of Palés Matos, when these two poets, each in his own manner, touched certain common chords. So

---

*The Puerto Rican national anthem, with music by Félix Astol and lyrics by Manuel Fernández Juncos. [Trans.]

too they lapped up the "popular" verses of Fortunato Vizcarrondo in which he reproached some Puerto Ricans (and how many of them there are!) for hiding grandmother in the kitchen *porque es prieta de verdá* ("because she's *so* black.")

Now of course it's true that the popularity of Vizcarrondo's poetry owed much to the wide coverage it received on radio and in the theatre as a result of the excellent recitations by Juan Boria, and that the poems of Lloréns and Palés enjoyed an ever-widening public once they had been included in the syllabus of Puerto Rico's public schools. For obvious reasons these advantages were denied to the seditious poems of Lola and Pachín during the Spanish colonial regime. But for all that, I think the basic reason why Lola and Pachín's revolutionary poetry never gained a following with the Puerto Rican masses lies in the difference between the ideological temperature of their poetry and that of the people. And I should make it clear that when I say "masses" I refer to the urban part of those masses. The rural parts, the countrymen who formed a demographic majority and lived in isolation from the country's cultural centers, certainly weren't alien to "*the*" culture, even though at the same time they were producing their own culture, which has so far only been studied as "folklore" — that is to say, from a point of view *external* to its own reality. But to return to the urban part, its ideological temperature last century reflected that of the creole ruling class in that it was reformist (i.e. autonomist) but not revolutionary (i.e. separatist), hence in no condition to assimilate the radical and subversive message expressed in the verses of Lola and Pachín. The political leaders of *these* masses were Muñoz Rivera and Barbosa rather than Betances and Hostos (both of whom had in any case been in political exile for a number of years).

Under the American colonial regime, when part of the creole ruling class found itself in conflict with the interests of the new metropolis, that same Muñoz Rivera together with José de Diego produced a patriotic poetry which achieved much greater popularity than anything written by Lola or Pachín, even though it never achieved unanimous or even near-unanimous acceptance. One reason for this last fact is that a considerable sector of the masses had already become republican or socialist, in other words as ideologically opposed to Muñoz Rivera as it was to José de Diego. Only in the 1930s, under the impact of an economic crisis that affected society as a whole, did an art of accusation and protest finally emerge that was "popular" in its forms and ideologically in tune with the masses, both urban and rural, in being reformist (though not exactly revolutionary). The "Lamento Borincano," in my opinion, was just such an art. In fact, it seems to me neither exaggerated nor untruthful to say that the true prophet (and remember that from "prophet" comes "prophecy") of the political movement headed at the end of the 1930s by Luis Muñoz Marín was Rafael Hernández. Such a fact and its implications for the situation today doubtless deserve more attention than there is space for here. Let them therefore await another occasion — or better still, pens more authoritative than mine.

(*1982*)

On Puerto Rican Literature
of the 1950s

The Puerto Rican literary panorama of the 1950s seems basically characterized by an undeniable boom in prose narrative, a theatrical revival virtually brought about by only two authors, and a relative decline in poetry and the essay forms which had dominated the country's literature for the previous two decades. (To thoroughly substantiate such a generalization would of course require a sedulous listing of more exceptions than this short essay can find space for.)

To start with, the division of literary history into decades is a riskier and more arbitrary undertaking than the old and no less questionable division into literary "generations." In the particular case of Puerto Rican literature, it has been the habit to identify "generations" with decades and even with five-year periods (the "Generation of the '30s," the "Generation of the '40s," the "Generation of forty-five," the "Generation of the '50s," the "Generation of the '60s," the "Generation of sixty-five," the "Generation of the '70s," — and God grant it won't be necessary to add etceteras to this in future!). Personally, I have ceased to believe in "literary generations," because these are invariably defined in terms of an outstanding *group*, within a whole generation that includes many writers of varied artistic and ideological persuasion. I believe even less in the existence of "literary periods," since they usually have more to do with the convenience of decimalization than with the complex realities of any cultural process.

To take an example: historians of Puerto Rican literature have never succeeded in agreeing about a chronological

91

description of the literary "generation" to which they claim I belong. The "Generation of the '40s," the "Generation of forty-five," the "Generation of the '50s" (which I myself put forward, only to reject it later for reasons I have given above), and finally the "Generation of the Second World War," are some of the periodizing categories so far proposed. But in fact, *all* of these are off the mark. A "Generation of the '40s" implies a common category for two such very different writers, to give just one example, as Wilfredo Braschi and Emilio Díaz Valcárcel; "Generation of forty-five" is a mere half-hearted compromise between "the '40s" and "the '50s"; "Generation of the '50s" allows us to include as important a writer as César Andreu Iglesias if we focus on when his books were published rather than on when he was born, but ignores the fact that Iglesias, one of the supposedly most representative short story writers of this "generation," published his first *three* books in the course of the previous decade (and it was I who thought up this label in the first place!); finally, "Generation of the Second World War" is worth about as much as, or perhaps less than, "Generation of the Korean War" since it fails to find a category for two writers who clearly belong to the same literary "generation," even though their first books appeared many years after these two wars: Edwin Figueroa and José Luis Vivas Maldonado.

The method of describing periods by "generations" inevitably leads — and to me this is its greatest drawback — to the contrived search for, and contrived discovery of, unreal homogeneities and even "group leaders," who in reality never existed. When the author of the most recent history of Puerto Rican literature asserts that René Marqués was the "spokesman" for the short story writers of the "Generation of forty-five," I can only feel myself excluded from such a presumed "generation," since it would be difficult to find in all contemporary Puerto Rican literature two writers with visions of the world and of their country, more diametrically opposed than Marqués and myself. (And, parenthetically, might I ask this particular student of our national literature, as well as all critics who comment on my work, to do me the favor not to attribute to me the authorship of a book entitled *El país de los cuatro pisos*? That *los* is not only grammatically superfluous and stylistically clumsy, but appears nowhere, not even as a misprint, in the title of my modest book of essays, as anyone who has even glanced at its cover can readily confirm.)*

I do not therefore intend to refer in what follows to the literary work of the "Generation of the '50s" or to any other rubric worthy of calendar art, but instead to certain characteristics in the literature produced in Puerto Rico between 1950 and 1959 that I consider important — clearly a concept very different from any of the labels I have just been discussing. (The true decade of course runs from 1951 to 1960, because as we all learned at primary school, one begins to count from *one* and not from *zero* — but then we all by now agree that I am in no sense a "decadist"!)

What I am interested in, above and beyond any other consideration that might be thought valid or useful in this particular case, is the relation I think I observe between the thematic and formal characteristics of the literature of this period and the socio-historical context in which it was conceived and nurtured. To begin with, I must say that I have never seen anything resembling a *rupture* between this literature and the national literary tradition as such. What I have always seen, and still see, is a thread of continuity between what was written in Puerto Rico from the time of Alejandro Tapia y Rivera and Manuel Alonso, to the time of

---

*The correct Spanish title is of course *El país de cuatro pisos*. [Trans.]

Emilio S. Belaval, J. I. de Diego Padró and Enrique A. Laguerre, by way of Manuel Zeno Gandía and Miguel Meléndez Muñoz — to mention only the most representative prose writers of the first hundred years of Puerto Rican literature. A thread of continuity doesn't of course mean that these writers adopted the same themes and forms; what it *does* mean is that they shared a common view as to what the *function* of literature should be in the historical development of their society. And as Dostoievsky recognized that all the Russian writers of his time — and how many, varied and magnificent they were too! — descended from Gogol's "The Cloak," so I venture to suggest (and making due allowance for obvious differences) that the Puerto Rican writers of my own time are the legitimate heirs of *El gíbaro, La Charca*, and *Cuentos para fomentar el turismo.*

To such progenitors our generation must add certain foreign godparents, such as Hemingway, Faulkner, Sartre and Silone — which only goes to confirm a similar proclivity on the part of another generation of Puerto Rican writers: we remember, for example, that Alonso was the disciple of Bretón de los Herreros, Zeno Gandía of Zola, and Belaval of Valle Inclán. However, to be indebted to a master isn't necessarily the same thing as to be a vassal to that master, and this also holds true for young Puerto Rican writers of today, who recognize the mastery of, to take but two examples, Julio Cortázar and Virginia Woolf. (Incidentally, it is high time critics and professors of literature stopped talking about *influences* and began talking about *affinities*, which is what it really amounts to in practice.) The essential continuity of our literary tradition, what is more, is assured by the fact that the best writers of the immediately preceding "generations" published some of their most important works in the 1950s. Examples that come to mind are the mature novels of Laguerre, the last stories of Tomás

Blanco, Palés Matos's splendid late poetry, and the already mature verses of Juan Antonio Corretjer and Francisco Matos Paoli.

As is well known, the early work of the young writers of those years — González, Soto, and Díaz Valcárcel in the chronological order of their appearance — introduced notable thematic and stylistic innovations. As far as thematic innovations are concerned, criticism has laid special emphasis on the way urban subjects replaced rural ones, and yet this, true as it is if one thinks of the earlier *"jibarista"* literature, can also be interpreted more readily as continuity than as rupture. As a matter of fact, the best nineteenth-century Puerto Rican fiction from Tapia y Rivera to Zeno Gandía took most of its subject matter from the towns (and it should also be remembered that of the four novels written by Zeno Gandía, only one, *La Charca*, has a rural setting, which moreover is not idealized in the novel but instead is criticized from a radically urban point of view). Even in the novels of the so-called "Generation of the '30s," supposedly telluric and *jibarista* by antonomasia, there is an indisputable preference for urban settings. And of the four books of stories by Emilio S. Belaval, three are set in Río Piedras and San Juan. After *La llamarada* and *Solar Montoya*, Laguerre focused on the countryside only in his novel *La resaca*, which moreover has a historical setting. Tomás Blanco and J. I. de Diego Padró were urban writers above all else.

Of what then does the much touted "urbanophilia" of the writers of the '50s really consist? Personally, what I have long believed is that all we did (and it certainly wasn't without its value) was to express in literary terms the reality of a *new type* of urban life in Puerto Rico. In this sense, we were and continue to be as attentive to Puerto Rican realities as our immediate or remote predecessors, but with an important difference: what they wrote about were towns in a

Puerto Rico in which most people still lived in the country and where consequently a majority of town dwellers still enjoyed a rural mentality, which largely determined their social and cultural attitudes, whereas René Marqués, Pedro Juan Soto, Díaz Valcárcel and I came to the realization that the society in which we lived had begun a process of irrevocable urbanization, with the rural population becoming displaced, not merely to urban centers on the island, but also to New York and other cities on the mainland. (This is particularly true of Marqués at the beginning of his career and before the notorious disenchantment with Puerto Rican reality of his later years made him turn to a pastoralism more romantic than realistic, ideologically speaking, but which can already be sensed in early works such as *La carreta*. As for Pedro Juan Soto, as is well known he had lived through the experience at first hand, as a emigrant to New York City.) Moreover, we felt that such a process of urbanization and emigration had necessarily engendered people and situations requiring new forms, as novel as the experiences they were meant to capture, before they could become incorporated into our literature. Obviously, living when he did, Manuel Zeno Gandía could not have created the crippled veteran of the Korean War that Emilio Díaz Valcárcel portrayed in "El sapo y el espejo," nor could the experiences of the protagonist of Zeno's *Redentores* have anything in common with the New York experiences of the protagonists of my own *Paisa*, or Pedro Juan Soto's *Spiks*.

I must now repeat what I said earlier, that those Puerto Ricans of a new social type could only express themselves in a Puerto Rican literature that had adopted a new subject matter and new forms, even though what *wasn't* new was the function of interpreting and criticizing reality in a way our predecessors, and we ourselves, thought necessary for a literature worthy of being called "national." The same, *mutatis mutandis*, can be said of Luis Rafael Sánchez,

Edgardo Rodríguez Juliá, Ana Lydia Vega and all our immediate successors, numerous and highly talented as they are. In this (which is the heart of the matter) there has been no essential change whatsoever. Where there *has* been a change is in the expressive techniques needed to turn our new individual and collective situations and attitudes into literature. I don't believe — and I hasten to say this in order to forestall any possible misunderstanding — that such a function must necessarily characterize, exclusively and eternally, Puerto Rican literature. I would very much like to see the day when my country's writers feel free to dedicate themselves to cultivating literature that is purely imaginative and even playful, without running the risk thereby of seeming to ignore the suffering of their fellow citizens. (I am speaking, of course, of a suffering which is the result of social injustice, because I fear that the other sort of suffering, which wells up from deeper and darker areas of human experience, will always be with us.) But however much I look forward to that day, I know very well it won't come in my lifetime. And yet so as to clear up any doubts on this particular subject, I declare that *I* won't be the one to condemn those who choose that other sort of literature, since it too in its particular way enriches human life in the here and now.

But let me now return to the immediate subject of this essay, which is the panorama of Puerto Rican literature in the 1950s. I want to (and should) say something at this point about the relative decline in poetry and the essay during this decade, but to do that I must first point to the defining characteristics of the social and political — and so cultural — milieu in which Puerto Rican writers then had to work. On another occasion I called those of us then engaged in creating the new Puerto Rican literature, "rebel sons of the Commonwealth." Now it won't be necessary to explain to any Puerto Rican reader the meaning of that last phrase,* but what he or she will have to be reminded of, in the hope that someone will feel inspired to examine the phenomenon with the attention it deserves, is that there was a complicated, problematic co-existence of two distinct elements within the Puerto Rican culture of the time: a McCarthyite intolerance, imposed from the metropolis, and a cautious cultural politics, both populist and "Puerto Ricanist," orchestrated by the insular government through the Institute of Puerto Rican Culture and the Division of Community Education. Both the Institute and the Division then functioned to a certain degree as politically calibrated counterweights to the "universalism" then being advocated within the purlieus of the University of Puerto Rico with the intention of reducing the national culture to a simple-minded and derisory "folklore." "Puerto Ricanists" and "universalists" rubbed shoulders within the government of the Popular Democratic party, and Luis Muñoz Marín, as undisputed chief and supreme arbiter both of party and government, chose to apportion official cultural power between both factions. In that way he not only quelled infighting, but he also created an image of cultural pluralism that allowed him to disarm his opponents' criticism, whether from the "left" or the "right." In answer to the leftists, he could point to the existence of the Institute of Puerto Rican Culture and the Division of Community Education, and in answer to the rightists, to the existence of the University. The historian who tries to draw up a balance sheet of such a situation will have to take into account, not only the deficiencies and ambiguities that in those years no doubt existed in the Institute of Puerto Rican Culture and the

---

*But non-Puerto Rican readers may wish to know the reference is to the *Estado Libre Asociado,* or "Commonwealth," which has been the island's official status since 1952. [Trans.]

Division of Community Education, but also the fact that many of the Puerto Rican writers and artists who were then producing their best work found employment — and in many cases moral asylum — in both institutions. (Editorial asylum as it affected writers was the contribution of the independent and indefatigable Nilita Vientos Gastón through the pages of her admirable magazine *Asomante,* among whose supporters, though without ideological commitment, was that same Institute of Puerto Rican Culture.)

The decade of the 1950s in Puerto Rican poetry will always be remembered for Luis Palés Matos's "Puerta al tiempo en tres voces," in my opinion the best lyric poem in the national literature, as also (as I have already pointed out), for a good part of the mature work of Matos Paoli and Corretjer. Nevertheless, the majority of those who began to write poetry during that decade were victims of a polarization between the ideologies of "transcendentalism" and "commitment" — a "transcendentalism" that in fact transcended very little because its aesthetic and philosophical bases were anything but original, and a "commitment" that never quite achieved the aim its spokesmen wanted, which was a marriage of politics and literature. The best of the "committed" poets was Hugo Margenat, for whom we had great hopes but who died before his unquestionable talent had had time to mature.

The Puerto Rican essay in this decade seems to have been overshadowed by the prestige of the two seminal contributions to the genre made by writers of the "Generation of the '30s," Antonio S. Pedreira's *Insularismo* and Tomás Blanco's *Prontuario histórico de Puerto Rico.* This prestige of course relied on the fact that these two books initially provided the ideological backing for the prolonged hegemony of the Popular Democratic Party, the political party that governed the colony for almost three decades. Pedreira and Blanco wrote their respective books from within the circles of power, but those who could have been their successors found that they had to trade in the lances of criticism for the trumpets of espousal, becoming more-or-less effective article-writers, but never graduating into essayists who dealt with ideas. The same must regretfully be said about their opponents, who confined themselves to ephemeral journalism or to parliamentary or commemorative speechifying. Essays of literary criticism, in particular academic essays, decorously survived, thanks to the continuing efforts of a group of teachers, whose most important works had already appeared years back, and to the first efforts of their students, whose mature work still lay in the future.

Puerto Rican theatre of the 1950s was virtually monopolized by René Marqués, then in the first stage of his career as a playwright. That "virtually" is a concession to the efforts of Francisco Arriví in the same genre. Even if the formal quality of Arriví's work isn't in my opinion comparable to the best of Marqués, still Arriví is the only important playwright of our times who has made the contentious and generally overlooked Puerto Rican problem of race the central theme of some of his pieces. It is as deplorable as it is significant that no one has had the necessary courage to follow him down this particular path, so little frequented, not only in our theatre, but in our literature as a whole. (The brilliant exception has been Carmelo Rodríguez Torres in the following generation.) The traditionalist and essentially conservative nationalism characterizing the ideology of the most representative — and most often represented — works by Rénè Marqués, expresses a vision of Puerto Rican reality that ignores the fundamental social conditions governing that society, namely class and race. Instead, Marqués pays deference to a patriotism that has eyes and ears only for "the tiger without," but remains blind and deaf to "the tiger within" — to quote the lucid and eloquent metaphor of José

Martí, which Arcadio Díaz Quiñones reminded us of only the other day.

I acknowledge that there remains much more to be said than what I have been able to say in this necessarily schematic essay. However, I hope there will be time and occasion in the future to continue filling in the inevitable gaps and omissions, some with my own thoughts and some with the thoughts of those others, fortunately every day more numerous, who keep me company in the task of interpreting and reinterpreting — which is to say building and rebuilding — the national culture that belongs to us all.

(1987)

Bernardo Vega: A Fighter and His People

No one could have seemed further from death, such being the force of his infectious vitality, than César Andreu Iglesias when he first spoke to me of these *Memorias de Bernardo Vega*. Neither Iglesias nor anyone else could have imagined that preparing this book for publication would be the last creative task that this veteran fighter for socialism and Puerto Rican independence would ever complete. The importance he ascribed to the job, which caused him to set aside at least two other projects that would have been first-rate contributions to our national heritage (a novel and a long essay on the national identity question), were more than justified by the intrinsic merits of Bernardo's manuscript, a text that, even beyond its claims as autobiography and as the narrative of an individual life (though that too was certainly worth the telling), constituted a quite exceptional contribution *to the history of the Puerto Rican community in New York,* as César himself realized and as he made clear in the book's subtitle. He also understood something that his legendary modesty prevented him from admitting even to his closest friends but that I must now make public for the sake of justice, which is that no other living Puerto Rican was as qualified as he himself was to *assume* the text and unreservedly identify himself with its rich human, political and moral subject matter. The explanation for such a fortunate circumstance — fortunate both for the book itself and for its readers — lies in the profound affinity between two lives that were both dedicated with exemplary single-mindedness to the same revolutionary cause.

The ideological trenches in which Bernardo Vega and César Andreu Iglesias fought throughout their militant careers stretched across the same far-flung terrain that that nation occupies which is divided between Puerto Rico and the great emigrant community living in the United States and particularly in New York. The strong insular roots in Bernardo never lost their vigor and for his part César never succumbed to the pettiness of denying Puerto Rican identity to the great transplanted emigrant mass. Faithful sons of the working class as they were, both Vega and Iglesias knew that the fatherland isn't an inherited property, as it is for the middle class, but an attainable possibility. This was the fundamental and lasting lesson I learned from both of them in my early youth. César knew that I owed them both a debt, but in what touched him personally the only payment he extracted was an unhesitating loyalty to the principles I had learned in his company. As for the debt to Bernardo Vega, when shortly before César's unexpected and premature death he asked me to write a few pages on Bernardo for inclusion in the *Memorias,* I realized that what he was doing was giving me the opportunity to begin paying that debt off. In fact, what follows goes well beyond the mere biographical memoir that César had in mind, but I know that he would have been pleased by my overcompliance with the task that he set me. And I also know that without a doubt Bernardo too would have been pleased, because in this attempt at providing an exegesis of his book he would have recognized the best possible tribute to his life as a militant.

I first got to know Bernardo Vega in 1947, just before the period when these *Memorias* end. Our personal friendship and political collaboration — in fact two inseparable aspects of one single human relationship — began, as he himself records it in this book, the day I joined the editorial staff of *Liberación,* the weekly which for several years was the incorruptible and militant defender of the Puerto Rican, Spanish, and Hispanoamerican communities in New York, or in other words, the organ of the *Hispanic* left in that great city that the author of the *Memorias* rightly calls *our* city. And if I italicize these two words *Hispanic* and *our*, it is because this emphasis focuses attention on an ideological issue of fundamental importance for the correct understanding of this autobiography, by one of the best sons of the Puerto Rican proletariat.

Again and again in these pages Bernardo alludes to the eminently popular character of the Puerto Rican emigration to the United States. This fact (which shouldn't surprise anyone, since it is well known that mass emigrations in the modern world are invariably caused by economic hardship, although I obviously exclude the massive albeit temporary migrations caused by natural disasters and by war), is something the author repeatedly points to in the context of a class-analysis of the Puerto Rican community in New York. With the precision and clarity that only this type of analysis can provide, Bernardo establishes the fundamental difference between the forced and hazardous *emigration* of the poor, and the voluntary *exile* of the rich, the latter only honorable when it involves a sacrifice of those riches on the altars of the struggle for freedom.

Our writer tracks down this distinction to its nineteenth-century origins using the reminiscences of his uncle Antonio, an exceptionally interesting figure, whose recollections throw light on some of the least studied aspects of our history. When we Puerto Ricans decide to analyze the thoughts and actions of our nineteenth-century separatists in the light of a *social* reality that determines and conditions all *ideological* expression, not only will we discover the true historical significance of a Betances, a Ruiz Belvis, and a Hostos — all anti-slavist, anti-racist, anti-monarchical, and anti-clerical, and *as a consequence* of all this, separatists — but we will also inevitably discover the essential historical difference between the revolutionary separatism last century and the conservative independentism that has impeded and objectively distorted our struggle for national emancipation this century. We will then be in a position to understand — and *must* understand, unless we wish to remain prisoners to an ideology both decrepit and unworkable — the hitherto unexplained contrast between the conservative and traditional Hispanophilia of a José de Diego or an Albizu Campos, and Betances's attitude, when he distributed coins to some children on the border between France and Spain and told them to shout "Viva Cuba libre!". (José Martí, whose presence is so pervasive in the *Memorias,* would surely have understood and applauded Betances for this act. On two well-known occasions he refused to enter a place where someone wanted to fly the Spanish flag. Bernardo Vega's uncle remembered one of these occasions and various biographers of The Apostle* have confirmed its authenticity. It happened when someone suggested that the Spanish flag should represent those Puerto Ricans present, at an event being celebrated by Antillean emigrants to New York. As for the other occasion, Martí himself refers to it in some verses from his *Versos sencillos*: "A dance! Let's go and see / The Spanish dancer. / They're right to take / The flag away; / If they had left it, / Well — I couldn't stay."†)

The *Hispanic* left to which Bernardo adhered obviously had nothing to do with the conservative Hispanophilia, with which he never had any sympathy. The Spain he *did* admire and defend was that *other* Spain, the populist and

---

*"The Apostle" was the name by which Martí was known to his admirers. [Trans.]

†"Hay baile; vamos a ver / La bailerina española. / Han hecho bien en quitar / El banderón de la acera; / Porque si está la bandera, / No sé, yo no puedo entrar."

democratic Spain that never held power here in Puerto Rico, nor alas, strictly speaking back in the home country either.) What it *did* derive from — and because of what follows I want to say this unambiguously — was Bernardo's recognition of a cultural and *social* community on which the Puerto Rican, Hispanoamerican, and Spanish workers living in New York could center their existence, more than on any other aspect of their collective identity. It is (or should be) clear that this *populist* Hispanicism of Bernardo Vega's has nothing at all to do with the conservative Hispanophilia, which has seen in the defense of a cultural patrimony denuded of all social content the reaffirmation of a link, not so much with the brother *peoples* of Spain and America, as with the hateful legacy of the Spanish colonial period. The Hispanics of New York were and continue to be a *people* and as such, as Bernardo rightly points out, are neither ashamed of their language nor of the Hispanic roots of their mestizo identity. Those who were in fact ashamed of those things were upper-class Puerto Ricans, the "respectable" Puerto Ricans who lived on Riverside Drive rather than in the Barrio and didn't dare read Spanish-language newspapers in public in case people accused them of being *spiks*, people "proud" of being Puerto Ricans in the bosom of their own class but careful to call themselves "Spanish" when they were with the arrogantly racist Americans. There is a passage in these *Memorias* where the division between these two groups of Puerto Ricans — between the *two fatherlands*, as any true socialist is bound to see it — can be noted with a dramatic clarity. The passage describes the occasion when more than a thousand Puerto Rican workers protested in front of the offices of a New York newspaper that had slandered them, while the millionaire Pedro Juan Serrallés *watched* the protest from the opposite sidewalk. "Yet again," as Bernardo Vega observes, "it fell to the workers to come to the defense of Puerto Rico."

"Yet again," because that is how it had been all through the nineteenth century, as Bernardo's uncle Antonio clearly remembers, when Cuban and Puerto Rican emigrant workers had supported the struggle for independence in both islands with what little money they had whereas the wealthy exiles had been niggardly to the point of meanness in their contributions to the cause. Who before Bernardo has described the cold welcome the Puerto Rican tobacco workers in New York at first gave the Puerto Rican Section of the Cuban Revolutionary party, founded by José Martí? Who has described or explained the reasons for this coolness? Of course historians of the creole bourgeoisie could not and cannot explain them, because those historians represented (and still represent) the same class interests as those who for the most part occupied positions of authority in the Section. However, Bernardo Vega *could,* because he had learned the facts from his uncle, a worker like himself, who had lived through the history *from below.* What is clear is that it needed the intervention of Sotero Figueroa, the lower-class mulatto newspaper-man who enjoyed Martí's complete confidence, for the impoverished Puerto Rican workers to overcome their natural suspicion of their compatriots from the other class.

Often when I have pointed out these facts to Puerto Rican independentists, who still think in terms of an abstract fatherland ideally uncontaminated by the class struggle, I have had to listen to and find an answer for the following objection: "But were not Betances, Ruiz Belvis and Hostos all members of the socially privileged class?" What in fact they *were* members of, as I have already explained, was the revolutionary sector of that class, in a period earlier by a generation than the period of Martí, Sotero Figueroa, Pachín Marín and Bernardo Vega's uncle Antonio. In that earlier period, the revolutionary sector of the creole bourgeoisie that I have referred to, faced with the indifference and even opposition of the reformist and assimilationist majority ofthe same class, attempted to break the colonial link with Spain. In this attempt they counted not on the majority of their own class, but on the support of the peons and slaves who fought at Lares under the leadership of the insurrectionary small landowners. (Betances himself more than once complained bitterly about being deserted by his class, as those who have read his correspondence will remember.) And after the defeat of this first attempt at revolution, the greater part of the Puerto Rican creole bourgeoisie opportunistically sought a *modus vivendi* with the Spanish monarchy, hoping thereby to gain a profitable role in the exploitation of their own country — which is to say, their own people. It wasn't "political skill" that this social class lacked; what it really lacked was any true sense of the nation together with a revolutionary ideology like that of the contemporary Cuban creole bourgeoisie, which is why Cuban revolutionary socialists today can see in the creole bourgeoisie's struggle against Spanish colonialism a historical antecedent for the anti-imperialism of their present-day struggle.

What lay behind the Agreement with Sagasta in 1898, then, was exactly what lay behind the creation of the *Estado Libre Asociado* or Commonwealth, in 1952: the historic opportunism of the Puerto Rican creole bourgeoisie and its inveterate propensity to strike a bargain with its imperial master. It is this that our bourgeois historians, whether patriots or non-patriots, have never wanted or been able to understand, but that Bernardo Vega understood perfectly well when, three decades ago, he wrote in his diary, "What a role my old friend Muñoz Marín is now playing! Every day he seems more like his father at the time of the Agreement with Sagasta!" And he understood it, not because he had the training of a professional historian, but because he had the insight of an enlightened proletarian.

It is lamentable, though no less explicable because lamentable, that many young Puerto Ricans with a revolutionary calling do not know these days the tradition of proletarian enlightenment so splendidly embodied in Bernardo Vega's thought and behavior. It is a tradition that, for all its nineteenth-century antecedents, was virtually born and grew to maturity in the first decades of this century. There are two fundamental reasons why this should have been so. The first is that under Spanish rule the limited economic development of Puerto Rico and the retrograde and oppressive character of the government prevented a modern working class from coming into being and with it an organized workers' movement, which might have influenced the country's social and political life; the second is that both these things, the relatively new working class and the organized workers' movement, were, relatively speaking, historical products of the American regime. But merely to state such a truth (no more than a commonplace for any beginning student of Marxism) has scandalized and continues to scandalize all bourgeois and petit-bourgeois patriots, who interpret it, through the warped historical vision of their class, as a justification, perhaps even apology, for the colonialism imposed on them by the United States. Such misunderstandings are, alas, common among many young independentists identifying with socialism in the Puerto Rico of today.

The explanation for such misunderstandings is grounded in a straightforward historical fact, which is that these young people's identification with socialism is a *subjective* identification. By this I mean that most of these young people do not hail from the working class, but instead from those sectors of the creole bourgeoisie, or creole petite bourgeoisie, that have been marginated by the American colonial regime. From that margination stems these young people's rebelliousness toward the colonial regime, and from their recognition that their own class is both unwilling and unable to oppose that regime stems their subjective identification with the working class and with what they take to be socialism. Let me make it clear, however, that I view these young people with sympathy and with hope. On them depends, at least in part, the future of socialism in Puerto Rico, since they are the ones who are really capable of bringing about the intellectual ferment that would help make the true Puerto Rican revolution viable in our time. But for that to happen, and for the revolution not to be frustrated or deformed by the weight of ideological concepts which are out-dated and essentially alien to socialism, it is essential that these young people *objectively* make their own the historical realities facing our country and the traditions of struggle associated with our working class. So too is it vital that they discard that *other* class tradition formed this century, the tradition of bourgeois and petit-bourgeois independentism that still weighs heavily on their shoulders. What is involved here is a genuine ideological catharsis, and for such a catharsis to work, the reading of these *Memorias de Bernardo Vega* will be an enormous help. In the *Memorias* these young people would find, as an account of actual experience, what we have just expressed in the form of an historical judgment:

> The workers' movement had acquired momentum in Puerto Rico under the new [American] regime. The affluent classes, especially the industrialists and wealthy farmers, felt that their interests were now threatened, hence the notorious proceedings against Santiago Iglesias and other workers' leaders, who were accused of "conspiring to raise wages." Iglesias was condemned to three years' imprisonment and his companions to varying penalties. The news of so great an outrage enraged the workers in New York. A

campaign was initiated in support of the workers'
leaders and in defense of the Free Federation of
Workers. . . .

All the bourgeois independentists have to say about this
Free Federation of Workers is that it was an instrument of
colonization on behalf of American imperialism in Puerto
Rico. This, although it contains a grain of truth, is certainly
not the whole truth. To discover the whole truth one would
first have to ask why American imperialism *could* use the
Free Federation of Workers as an instrument of colonization.
The judicial proceedings against Santiago Iglesias and his
companions, mentioned by Bernardo Vega, can set us on the
way, as few other facts can at that particular historical
moment, to the discovery of an answer to this question.
Iglesias and his followers were prosecuted by a Puerto Rican
district attorney before a Puerto Rican judge by virtue of a
Spanish law that described all strikes for better wages as
"crimes of conspiracy." This was the social legislation in
force in Puerto Rico under the Spanish colonial regime and
this was the legislation that the Puerto Rican attorney and
the Puerto Rican judge, who sent Iglesias and his companions
to jail, accepted as binding after the end of Spanish
sovereignty in Puerto Rico. When the case reached the
Puerto Rican Supreme Court on appeal, the Attorney General
of the new regime, an American named Harlan, wrote a
letter to the district attorney of that court, which near the
end says the following: "The right to assemble peaceably for
mutual consultation and for joint endeavour in an orderly
manner to better social conditions is surely fundamental. If
any Spanish law in Porto Rico . . . impairs this right, in my
judgment it has lost its force and become a nullity with a
change of sovereignty. Such a law is contrary to the spirit of
our form of government." The district attorney of the
Supreme Court, now knowing what was expected of him,

acceded to the petition for an acquittal, which the defending advocate had submitted. Who can be surprised, then, that Puerto Rican workers felt themselves protected and defended by the new regime? And who can be surprised that the regime, understanding this feeling, should use it to its own political advantage? What would really have been surprising would have been any other outcome.

Seeing matters in this light (and there seems to be no better light in which to see them), who can claim to find it *historically* culpable that the Puerto Rican workers' movement this century was corrupted by American influence? The bourgeois independence movement has traditionally pointed its finger at two culprits, Santiago Iglesias and American imperialism. Evidently neither of them can be wholly absolved. But then what *historical reality* made possible the success both had in working upon the feelings of the Puerto Rican working class? Neither Iglesias nor American imperialism had created that historical reality. Without a doubt, it was the Spanish colonial regime that had created it and nothing corroborates this better than what Eugenio María de Hostos wrote about the situation Puerto Rican society found itself in at the moment of the so-called "change of sovereignty."*

"When one looks at Puerto Rico in the dim light of a new life that is now dawning," wrote the great Puerto Rican patriot on returning to the island in 1898, "it seems as though everything in that life is hostile to the humane objectives of the *League* [*of Patriots*]. The island's population is totally impoverished. Physiological and economic misery go hand in hand. The malarial fever that mummifies the individual is

---

*All quotations from Hostos that follow are taken from *Madre Isla*, volume V of *Obras completas* (Cultural S.A., La Habana, 1939). The page number from this edition follows each quotation.

mummifying society as a whole. Those half-moving skeletons on the coastal plains and in the mountains, who give proof of how systematic the colonial regime has been in its policy of *mass relocations*; that feeble childhood; that sunken-chested adolescence; that withered youth; that sicklied manhood; that premature old age, in short that individual and social debility everywhere visible, seem to have rendered our people incapable of helping themselves" (pp. 26–27). "If for some reason [*The League of Patriots*] collapses one day, it will be because of the inertia of the Puerto Ricans, because of the terrible fact that the Spanish domination has left them so passive that they do not even have the energy or initiative to make themselves into a real people" (p. 24).

But it wasn't only the popular masses who were in such a state of prostration; it was also the intellectual élite, from whom so much was then to be expected: "Because they have been so corrupted by colonialism, not even the most educated men in Puerto Rico (and there are many more of them than patriotism has the right to expect after so disastrous an occupation as the Spanish), not even the most educated men in Puerto Rico can make up their minds to take any initiative, or wholly rely on themselves, or cease to hope that their government will solve all their problems. Since what is needed today is just the opposite . . . our society must acquire the two sources of energy colonialism has deprived it of, when it inhibited the exercise of those rights that strengthen in the individual both his private energies and his energies in association with other people" (pp. 13–14).

Taking all this into account (and can there be any Hispanophile "patriot" who dares accuse Hostos of falsifying the historical truth?), is it fair to accuse Puerto Rican workers in the first half of this century, as many have done who never knew the material and moral misery in which the Spanish colonial regime left those workers, of "lacking national feeling?" Nonetheless, twenty-nine years after a representative of American imperialism released from jail the strikers accused under a Spanish law of conspiracy, Pedro Albizu Campos asserted at a meeting of the Nationalist Party in Mayagüez: "In the United States a small minority or ruling class exploits virtually the whole country. There is no society there or nation in the strict sense of the word, but instead a vast conglomeration, which suffers the oppression of a tiny oligarchical class for whom the welfare, still less the betterment, of the masses doesn't matter in the least. By contrast, a homogeneity existed in Puerto Rico between all the classes, together with an acute sense that people should offer one another reciprocal help to strengthen and conserve the nation — in other words, a rooted and unanimous sense of fatherland. As a consequence, to set in class warfare the man who has nothing against the man who enjoys a modest income was to introduce an alien element of discord into our society."

What the nationalist leader told the Puerto Rican workers in 1931 — at the very moment when the world crisis of capitalism was intensifying the class struggle in all four corners of our planet! — was that the creation of a workers' movement in Puerto Rico had been unnecessary and harmful, because there had never been a class struggle on the island. According to Albizu, what *had* existed was a "homogeneity" between rich and poor, where people offered one another "reciprocal help" to "strengthen and conserve the nation," so that for the Puerto Rican workers to organize in defense of their class interests constituted "an alien element of discord" and was utterly superfluous. According to this curious "sociology" of Albizu's, if a workers' movement could be justified in the United States it was because in that country there was neither society nor nation, but merely "a vast conglomeration." (How the existence of a workers' movement could be justified in all those societies and nations which *weren't* merely "conglomerations" was something that Albizu's "social science" never took the trouble to explain.) We Puerto Ricans, by contrast, were a true nation, in which all people, rich and poor, were brothers and so obliged to help one another defend the nation, of which we were all, supposedly, owners-in-common in a sort of giant co-operative or limited partnership.

But the Puerto Rican workers knew, as a result of experience and by means of a sort of elemental class instinct, that what Albizu said wasn't in fact true. They knew that Albizu's mythical and mystical fatherland had never really existed and that the real Puerto Rican society had been, and continued to be, a society divided into classes. They knew that there had been, and continued to be, Puerto Ricans who were exploited and Puerto Ricans who did the exploiting. And they rightly told themselves that the independence to which Albizu referred was an independence based on ignoring or concealing that reality. They knew that at the same time that Albizu campaigned for the expulsion of the American exploiters from Puerto Rico (exploiters whom the workers knew very well, as is obvious from the way they mounted strikes against them), he was simultaneously affirming that we should "attempt to revive that multiplicity of proprietors that we had in 1898." They knew, by virtue of an experience that no rhetoric or fantasizing "sociology" could refute, that the law by which the strikers of 1902 had been condemned as "conspirators" was a law created to defend the interests of those same proprietors. They knew that Albizu was falsifying history when he described Puerto Rican society before 1898 as "the old collective happiness." At the very moment Albizu uttered these words, there were educated workers in Puerto Rico, workers in no sense antagonistic to the idea of national independence, who had read Manuel Zeno Gandía and knew that his description of that society as "a sick world" was closer to the historical truth than the description the nationalist leader was offering them.

Bernardo Vega was one of those educated workers. A tobacco worker by trade, as he often recalls with a justified pride in his *Memorias*, he belonged to the most cultivated and alert sector of the Puerto Rican proletariat. He was a member of the Free Federation of Workers and co-founder of the Socialist Party. Never deceived by the true nature of the American colonial regime in Puerto Rico, for four decades Vega struggled against it and in support of independence. But the independence he fought for was not, nor could ever be, the same independence the creole bourgeoisie, displaced from economic and political power as a result of the development of dependent capitalism in Puerto Rico, were in favor of. Men like Vega never found a place in the Nationalist Party, for the simple reason that it was never possible to fight in that party for both independence *and* the rights of the working class. (As a matter of fact, the only "leaders" the nationalists offered the Puerto Rican workers were the "men of stature"* they themselves had chosen!)

It was men like Bernardo Vega who in 1934 founded the Puerto Rican Communist party — on the anniversary of the Grito de Lares, as a matter of fact — in which it was not only possible, but mandatory, to fight simultaneously on both fronts, the nationalist and the socialist. But the nationalist movement always condemned these Puerto Rican communists as "divisionists," who "weakened" the struggle against the colonial regime by acting as the party of a separate class. The undeniable truth is that the communists always pursued a politics of alliance with *all* pro-independence groups, hoping thereby to create an alliance which would constitute an authentic national front of all classes and so unite under a

---

hombres de talla: a class term implying a degree of affluence and social acceptability. [Trans.]

single banner the entire spectrum of anti-colonial Puerto Rican society. The Nationalist Party rejected such a politics since it saw *itself* as representing the nation in its entirety (which is what the party's self-definition, as "the fatherland organized for the rescue of its sovereignty," really meant, with the implication that whoever didn't belong to the Nationalist Party didn't really belong to the fatherland either). Such an unrealistic way of seeing things not only made the creation of a nationalist anti-colonial front impossible, but led the Nationalist Party itself to an isolation that a few years later brought it to the very verge of extinction.

Bernardo Vega lived, at the heart of the Puerto Rican community in New York, through these political differences between nationalists and communists, and he gives an account of them in the *Memorias* that is particularly valuable for its frankness. The conflict, in fact, was already under way when Albizu Campos joined the Nationalist Party, which among other things proves that Albizu Campos's nationalism, far from being the creation of one man, embodied a true class ideology. Bernardo describes how in September 1923 the Workers' Alliance staged a meeting during which two of those present attacked the workers' organizations as "societies without a soul" and lacking all "sense of nationality" and "love for things of the spirit." As one of these critics put it: "All they seem to want for the workers is a hunk of bread." However, it was only in the 1930s that the discord reached a new pitch of virulence. Bernardo describes it as follows:

> About this time an unhappy incident muddied the waters of fraternal accord between Puerto Rican communists and nationalists. The nationalists expected Puerto Ricans, wherever they lived, to give all their enthusiasm and support to the struggle for independence

and went so far as to argue that to get involved in the immediate social struggles in New York was to divert Puerto Ricans from their primary patriotic task. In their opinion, Puerto Ricans weren't emigrants but rather "exiles," and as such their only thought should be for the redemption of their homeland and their own prompt return to Puerto Rico. The Puerto Rican workers, and in particular the communists and their sympathisers, rejected this position. For them the need to fight for the independence of Puerto Rico was beyond question, but that was no reason to stand by passively when faced with the exploitation of Puerto Ricans in New York. For them, what deserved priority was the immediate struggle. As long as these two opposing viewpoints only met at the level of debate, there was no immediate problem. But it was now that Puerto Rican nationalists and communists began to question each other's positions at street meetings one or the other group held in the Barrio Latino. The audience interrupted speakers with questions and this gave rise to the accusation that attempts were being made to "wreck" the meeting. So it was that both sides took to street fighting, that degenerated into hand-to-hand battles. The Puerto Rican nationalist Angel María Feliú was killed in one of these scuffles and the communists were accused of the crime.

When in 1946 I arrived in New York, people still remembered this tragic event, but by then relations between nationalists and communists had greatly improved — to such an extent, in fact, that collaboration in specific activities was now the order of the day. The nationalist leadership did not officially approve of this collaboration and even went so far as to expel some militants from the party for taking part in joint activities with the communists; moreover it continued to see Puerto Ricans in New York as "exiles" rather than as emigrants. But the realities of life, which bore on all with equal rigor, and the support that the communists always offered the nationalists, including Albizu Campos himself, when they were persecuted, ended by persuading most of the nationalists to take an active part in those social struggles in the community that the communists directed.

That a collaboration which couldn't yet take place in Puerto Rico took place in New York can only be explained by reference to the social composition of the emigrant community. This community, as we have already said and as everyone knows, was and continues to be overwhelmingly proletarian. The nationalism of Albizu Campos, which expressed the ideology of the marginated sector of the creole bourgeoisie and petite bourgeoisie, was for obvious reasons never to make any headway among the Puerto Rican proletariat, in either social or political terms. Any nationalist who was shackled to the ideology of the anti-American creole bourgeoisie in Puerto Rico began inevitably to become proletarianized as soon as he emigrated to the United States. Such a process made for conflicts in social, political, and psychological terms — conflicts, let it be said in passing, that comprise a quarry of topics that have yet to be exploited in our literature. The typical nationalist of the 1930s and '40s, a descendant of the ruined landowners of former times, found himself on the same social level in New York as a compatriot descended from peons and perhaps even slaves, American society showing no willingness to give him back those class privileges that had been recognized by the society back in Puerto Rico. Even those who were sufficiently well educated to see no reason why they should work in kitchens or factories often had to settle for jobs with salaries much closer to those of their proletarian compatriots than to the salaries of the better-paid sectors of the American petite bourgeoisie. On the other hand (and this is something we should in no way deny or underestimate), the nationalist emigrant, because of his intense patriotism, tended as a matter of course to live in close touch with his fellow countrymen. With them he shared a basically similar cultural tradition and a basically similar national psychology, so that with them, in the long or short run, he also came to share a social conscience that had seemed to him back in Puerto Rico (to use the words of his leader) "an alien element of discord."

A proletarian with a sense of nation like Bernardo Vega knew that the situation of the Puerto Ricans in New York had a lot to do with the colonial condition of Puerto Rico, but the historical experience of his class also told him that the problem was not merely colonial but also, and fundamentally, social. The exact expression of this truth is contained in three bare but eloquent sentences in the *Memorias*:

> On May 12 1942, after the formalities of an exam, I was accepted as a low-grade clerk, something that didn't disturb me. As a Puerto Rican, I well knew that it was my destiny to be an unskilled workman. . . . Such was the fate that we suffered under the Spanish and such is the fate, unchanged to the present day, that we now have to suffer under the Yankees.

There are two phrases in this passage that we must examine more closely to extract their full and instructive significance. The menial work assigned to Bernardo (during the Second World War he worked in the censorship bureau of the American Post Office) was "something that didn't disturb me." But how that same discrimination *would* have disturbed a middle-class Puerto Rican patriot, convinced of the superiority of his "race" and "Greco-Roman heritage," over the "coarse" and "utilitarian" Anglo-Saxon conception of life! However, for a socialist proletarian like Bernardo Vega discrimination was a daily fact and the inevitable corollary of an unjust social system, something that one had to struggle against, but which there was no need to be personally, which is to say subjectively, humiliated by.

The other phrase refers to the fate of Puerto Ricans as "unskilled workmen," as much "under the Spanish" as "under the Yankees." This comparison of the *two* colonial regimes, which Bernardo advances without feeling the need to supply a gloss, is irreconcilable with the traditional Hispano-philia of the Puerto Rican bourgeois independence movement, or with Albizu Campos's description of the Spanish colonial regime as "the old collective happiness." (And I say *irreconcilable* for the benefit of those who dream there could be some "fusion" of bourgeois nationalism and proletarian socialism in the Puerto Rico of today.)

If Bernardo knew that his destiny "as a Puerto Rican" would have made him an unskilled laborer under Spanish colonialism, it was because he never belonged to the *class* of Puerto Ricans who in 1896 came to an agreement with the Spanish monarchy to share the perquisites of exploiting that *other class* of Puerto Ricans, who had never been landowners, who had never felt themselves to be "Spaniards of the New World," and whose one possible accommodation with what Betances called "the stepmother country" — oppressive, exploitative, and discriminatory like every other imperial power — could only have taken the form of outright rejection. (As for the *other* Spain — popular, democratic and revolutionary — Bernardo Vega certainly felt solidarity with *that*. Hence his insistence that we take note that three hundred Puerto Ricans had fought to defend the Spanish Republic when it was attacked by General Franco's "nationalists" and the forces of international fascism. And this at the very moment when the Puerto Rican Nationalist Party refused to take sides in the struggle, because to take sides would have been to support one of the two factions into which "the mother country," i.e. Spain, had been "divided"!)

Who, if not a Puerto Rican working man with a sense of history, could call the city of New York *our* city? A fatherland for Bernardo Vega was never an unhistorical myth, never the mystical vision of an élite, but rather a human and social reality, actual and alive. A fatherland is a community of men and women who through an extended historical process have shaped a way to live their lives that is always responsive to change and evolution. Such change and evolution never intimidated Bernardo — in fact, very much the opposite since throughout his life he lived both *with* and *in* such evolution and such change. It was this that made it possible for him to see a reality that many intellectuals of the creole bourgeoisie are still blind to: the appearance and crystallization of a distinctive way of being Puerto Rican, in certain respects similar to the insular way but in other respects different. As he says:

> The Barrio Latino was acquiring its own special characteristics. A distinctive culture began to coalesce, based on the common experience of a population that had continually survived in spite of the hostility of its surroundings. In the long run this culture would bear its own special fruits.

As I have already said, there are still those who deny Puerto Ricanness to those fruits, perhaps because they do not notice that where Puerto Ricanness is really lacking is in the cultural and moral hybridism of the *other* "emigration," that of the rich Puerto Ricans whose only real fatherland is their bank account. Bernardo knew all that perfectly well, but even more noteworthy is his perception that this phenomenon wasn't merely to be found under the American colonial regime but could also be found, and to no lesser extent, under the regime that preceded it, the regime the bourgeois and Hispanophile nationalists continued to idealize and to enshrine in myth:

> I read in the San Juan papers that wealthy Puerto Ricans are investing their money in Florida. They mention Serrallés, Roig, Ramírez de Arellano, García Méndez, and Cabassa. . . . Every day I become more and more convinced that the capitalist class in Puerto Rico isn't really rooted in its native soil. The wealthy classes yesterday were Spanish. Today they are American. In the sin lies the penance!

In the sin lies the penance. It is the rich Puerto Ricans of yesterday and today who have committed the sin, but it is the poor Puerto Ricans who have suffered and continue to suffer the penance. Because, if the creole bourgeoisie's incapacity to fulfill its historic task still keeps our necks bowed under the colonial yoke, then strictly speaking, those who suffer the weight of that yoke are the eternally dispossessed, both those who remain on the island and those who have had to leave. It is for them — and for them only — now to lead the struggle toward the completion of this double task: our national emancipation and the destruction for good of a social regime founded on man's exploitation of man. Among all the lessons contained in this posthumous book by Bernardo Vega, none is as timely or as important as the lesson that points the way forward to our total liberation as a people.

(1977)

The Writer in Exile

Literally, I am not exaggerating when I say that my exile began in my mother's womb. Let me explain what I mean. My father, a Puerto Rican, married a Dominican when he was living in Santo Domingo and it was there that I was born, exactly fifty years ago. My father could never get used to the instability and violence of life in our Caribbean sister republic and so in the year of my birth, 1926, he tried another move, this time to New York where his mother and three younger brothers were already established. My mother and I remained in Santo Domingo and it wasn't long before my father returned there himself after having been mugged in the middle of a New York street. (Years later he told me that when he returned, the stab wound on his thigh hadn't yet healed.) After this, exile became for him an intolerable burden. In fact, my first childhood memory is of walks down by the Santo Domingo docks, where my father had taken me to see the ships leaving for Puerto Rico. It was on one of those ships, which my mother remembers was called the *Catherine* and registered in the United States, that we all left for Puerto Rico at the end of 1930. This was the same year that two disasters, very different in character but similar in their effects, scourged the Dominican people: the San Zenón hurricane and the rise to power of Rafael Leónidas Trujillo.

The word "exile" was to cast its evil shade over my entire childhood in Puerto Rico. Through our house (or rather, through the succession of houses we successively occupied during those difficult years of economic crisis) passed a variety of exiles from the Trujillo regime, all of whom invariably received a warm welcome. These were the "expelled," some of whom chose to put down roots in Puerto Rico whereas others stayed only a few months before re-embarking for Cuba or Venezuela. I was too young then to understand that this forced emigration represented, among other things, the political bankruptcy of an entire social class, the creole oligarchy which until then had administered and usufructed the country, essentially as a family holding. These were the so-called *gente decente* (decent people) of the country — also called the *gente bien* (nice people) or *gente distinguida* (distinguished people): lawyers, doctors and landowners, whose hegemony in Dominican society was founded upon a sort of hereditary right, but whose apparently incorrigible propensity for factional in-fighting had finally exasperated those American interests that required a measure of political and social stability in the country. It was that exasperation that led first of all to the American military occupation of Santo Domingo, and later to the establishment of a dictatorship led by a *caudillo* of plebeian origins, who committed himself to guarantee the order required by the imperial master: Rafael Leónidas Trujillo.

After a few years, the "order" of Trujillo's regime began to produce a new type of exile: the middle-class intellectual, who could not resign himself to the sterile choice between oligarchic anarchy and military despotism. One of these new exiles was the man who definitively set my incipient literary career on course when he reached Puerto Rico in 1938, Juan Bosch, the son of a Catalan immigrant and a transplanted Puerto Rican woman, who had settled as farmers in the fertile region of Cibao. Even though he was still very young, he was known as the best short story writer in his country and when he got to Puerto Rico at the age of thirty he was already master of the genre. From him I learned (as I have recorded elsewhere) that the best literature is a literature that succeeds in recreating life in all its concrete immediacy. He also taught me that in certain circumstances exile can prove a very effective form of service to one's country.

In 1946, eight years after having got to know Bosch, I left Puerto Rico for the first time. I had already published two books of stories, which critics said were like nothing previously written on the island. (And many good things *were* being written as anyone knows who has read the stories of Emilio S. Belaval and the novels of Enrique A. Laguerre. — but then I had inherited from Bosch a devotion to the best writer of short stories in the language, the Uruguayan Horacio Quiroga.) In New York, where I spent a year-and-a-half taking a master's degree in political science and another year-and-a-half pursuing a quite instructive variety of jobs, I discovered, with a fascination and respect that have stayed with me to this day, the existence of the Puerto Rican diaspora. That emigration, which today amounts to more than a million human beings (three million still living on the island), represents one of the major milestones of the Puerto Rican national experience. There is no aspect of the life of the Puerto Rican people this century — social, economic, political, cultural and psychological — that is not marked by the vicissitudes of this mass exodus. And what makes it different from other emigrations is that it is characterized by a constant coming and going from the home country to the seat of exile and vice-versa. This continuous flow has given rise to a phenomenon which is also of great interest: the maintenance of an extraordinarily strong link between the exiled community and the community that stayed at home.

But at the same time such a link is dramatically conflictive. The Puerto Rican who has emigrated and been rejected by a racist American society seizes hold of his national identity as the only means to spiritual survival, both personal and collective. But in spite of this, there are some Puerto Ricans at home who are fearful of the "foreignizing influences" that the emigrants can inflict on the "parent" society, with the result that they often reject the emigrants with a cruelty only to be explained by their own insecurity — which is itself the fruit of a colonial upbringing.

From my own New York experience came at least four literary texts: the short novel *Paisa* and the stories "En Nueva York," "El pasaje" and "La noche que volvimos a ser gente." Of these, only the last, I think, is on the level of the stories written by another author of my generation, Pedro Juan Soto, whose *Spiks* is the best book written in Spanish on the Puerto Rican emigration to the United States. And I say "Spanish" quite deliberately, because as early as the 1940s I believed (and said) that the most authoritative literary expression of Puerto Rican emigrants to the United States would one day have to be produced by their descendants — in English. (I should add that Pedro Juan Soto's parents were emigrants and that he lived his adolescence and early youth in New York; I by contrast was never an emigrant in any strict sense.) But literary works in English by the descendants of Puerto Rican emigrants to the United States now exist and they cause much perplexity to island intellectuals. Should they be considered "Puerto Rican literature" or should they not? For those who think that the national character of a literature depends primarily on the language it is written in, the answer is obviously no. But for those of us who think that the essential in a literature is the way it expresses a national reality, then the answer is equally obviously yes.

However, what those who deny national status to the literature written by English-speaking Puerto Ricans in the United States tend to forget is that these emigrants aren't the first Puerto Ricans to have written books in a language which isn't the language of a majority of Puerto Ricans. Allor almost all of the specifically literary works of Ramón

Emeterio Betances (recognized by all supporters of Puerto Rican independence as the Father of the Nation) were written in French and this for two easily comprehensible reasons: first, because Betances had been educated in France from his youth and was thus "Frenchified" in the best sense of the word, and second, because he so hated Spain for oppressing his own nation that he felt no special affection for the language of what he often called "the stepmother country." And Julia de Burgos, so far this century's most famous Puerto Rican woman poet, wrote her last poems, during her New York exile and not long before her premature death, in *English*. Betances and Julia de Burgos were of course exceptions. But then why not accept, in addition to these exceptions, the literary expression of a minority, written in a foreign language, within the body of the national literature? In my opinion, such an acceptance would represent an enrichment and not an unseemly capitulation.

What I want to say clearly, so as to avoid all misconceptions, is the following: I am proposing not a "concession" to this community but an acknowledgment of its rights, for the truth is that those who *had* to go, went, whereas those who stayed were those who *could* stay. By what social or moral right do the latter now presume to pass judgment on the "Puerto Ricanness" of the former? (However, I fear that a certain breed of nationalism, fatally limited by its class origins, will never be able to understand this sort of reasoning.)

But to return now to my subject. In the summer of 1950, soon after returning from the United States by way of Mexico — a Mexico I had just discovered for the first time and with a true delight — I headed off for Europe with the idea of spending a few weeks in Czechoslovakia as the Puerto Rican delegate to a world student conference. The nationalist uprising in Puerto Rico in October of the same year and thewave of political repression it unleashed forced me to prolong my stay in Europe for another two years. During that time I didn't stop writing, first in Prague and later in Paris, remembering that Eugenio María de Hostos, the greatest of our writers, had written most of his books away from Puerto Rico. And thinking of Hostos made me also think of Lola Rodríguez de Tio and Francisco Gonzalo Marín, both of whom produced their most mature work in political exile. I thought, too, of the Puerto Rican students of the *Grupito Criollo*, or Little Creole Group, who in mid-nineteenth-century Barcelona virtually brought our national literature into being, and of Tomás Blanco, who eighty years later in Madrid wrote his memorable and indispensable *Prontuario histórico de Puerto Rico*. Remembering these and so many other writers in the same predicament, I told myself that if destiny had singled me out to be another Puerto Rican writer in exile, then there was at least no reason for me to feel alien to what had become indeed a truly national destiny.

And that destiny was also to be mine, for when in mid-1952 I returned to Puerto Rico, then at the height of the Cold War and of McCarthyism, I found I could only stay a few months. And so in February 1953 I left for Mexico by way of Havana, sombre and tense because of Batista's new dictatorship, and thereby began my major period of exile, which has continued now for almost twenty years. Several commentators on what might charitably be called my literary oeuvre have referred to this exile as "voluntary" and if their use of this adjective is merely the result of not knowing the facts, then I readily forgive them. But the truth of the matter is that those many years in Mexico (and this isn't the first time I say this) have been more a *change* of country than a *loss* of country, more a *transtierro* than a *destierro*. In Mexico I continue to be a Puerto Rican writer, but have in addition become a teacher at a Mexican university, two circumstances that, far from being mutually exclusive, complement one another perfectly.

And yet in 1954, when I published a new book of stories in Mexico, some Puerto Rican critics were up in arms because two of these stories didn't deal with "Puerto Rican subjects." People then began to call me "uprooted" and to forecast my imminent literary demise. On another occasion I have spoken of those who saw "uprootedness" in my writing about "foreign" people and events, as symptomatic of that old nationalist prejudice which holds that a writer's national identity is exclusively determined by the geographical setting of his subject matter. This ingenuous belief totally ignores the fact that a writer's national roots aren't necessarily or essentially to be found in the characters or setting of his work, but rather in his own self and in his distinctive vision of reality, whatever that reality might be. Did Shakespeare cease to be English and become an Italian when he write *Romeo and Juliet*? Did Valle Inclán renounce his Spanishness when he wrote *Tirano Banderas*? Did Alejo Carpentier become a Haitian writer when he published *El reino de este mundo*?

This primitive nationalism of many Puerto Rican intellectuals, a nationalism Antonio S. Pedreira called "insularism," has of course an historical explanation and one that even Pedreira himself didn't fully perceive. It is, in fact, a nationalism appropriate to a particular class (as indeed are all nationalisms), the class in this case being the creole bourgeoisie, who in 1898 had made a bargain with Spain and thereby agreed to accept an autonomy more symbolic than real, but from 1898 on began to see themselves displaced as the ruling class in Puerto Rican society by the irruption of an imperialist American capitalism and its social and political concomitants. The resistance of this class to the new colonial master expressed itself culturally in an idealization of the past, which finished by stranding that class in a conservatism incapable of understanding, and consequently of evaluating, the transformations that had been taking place in their society for three quarters of a century. The political expression of this resistance — the twentieth-century independence movement, burdened by a conservative ideology which radically distinguishes it from the progressive separatism of the last century — has suffered from the same inability to understand the national condition. And as a result, this same independence movement (in fact the ideological spokesman for a class in full historical retreat) has found it can never win sufficient support from the masses to enable it to unleash a truly effective anticolonial struggle.

What such a situation naturally requires is the re-examination of the national condition from the foundations up. This is no easy task and the writer who from exile and favored by distance learns to contemplate the forest of such a national condition stumbles inevitably, once back in Puerto Rico, over the concern with individual trees that preoccupies so many of his contemporaries. Perhaps in the long run both focuses are necessary for a fruitful synthesis, and knowing this may help us maintain a just perspective on any apparently insuperable disagreements that may arise along the way. Certainly, without such knowledge the exile will have failed to learn the major lesson afforded him by his destiny.

(1976)

Glossary of Names

(All persons are Puerto Ricans unless otherwise stated.)

ALONSO, Manuel A. (1822–1889). Writer, doctor and journalist. His best-known work is *El gíbaro* (1849), a "Description of Customs in the Island of Puerto Rico."

ALBIZU Campos, Pedro (1891–1964). The leading nationalist leader this century, repeatedly imprisoned for his complicity in armed revolts against the American regime.

ANDREU Iglesias, César (1915–1976). Journalist and labor leader, one of the founders of the Movimiento Pro-Independencia in 1959.

BALDORIOTY de Castro, Ramón (1822–1889). Deputy to the Spanish Cortes, who campaigned for the abolition of slavery and for autonomy for Puerto Rico. First president of the Autonomist Party.

BARBOSA, José Celso (1857–1921). Mulatto doctor and member of the Autonomist Party. In 1899 he founded the Puerto Rican Republican Party and later campaigned for Puerto Rico to become a state of the Union.

BETANCES, Ramón Emeterio (1827–1898). Mulatto doctor and fearless campaigner for independence and the abolition of slavery. Involved in the Lares uprising (1868) and later exiled to France.

BLANCO, Tomás (1900–1975). Author and essayist. His best-known work is *Prontuario histórico de Puerto Rico* (1935).

BRAU, Salvador (1842–1912). Essayist, journalist, historian. His best-known work is his *Historia de Puerto Rico* (1904).

133

CAMPECHE, José (1751–1809). Portrait painter and Puerto Rico's first major visual artist.

DE DIEGO, José (1866–1918). Politican and poet. Co-founder of the Partido de la Union de Puerto Rico (1904). He shifted his political position more than once, but at the end of his life was pro-independence and in favor of an Antillean Union.

FIGUEROA, Sotero (1863–1923). Mulatto. Supporter first of autonomy, then of independence. Editor of "Patria," José Martí's newspaper in New York City.

HENRÍQUEZ, Miguel (early 18th century). Mulatto shoemaker who became a corsair and later the captain of a Spanish warship. Helped reconquer Vieques (1717).

HERNÁNDEZ, Rafael (1892–1965). Composer of popular songs of worldwide renown.

HOSTOS, Eugenio María de (1839–1903). Writer, educationalist, and lifelong advocate of Puerto Rican independence. His best-known literary work is the novel *La peregrinación de Bayoán* (1863).

IGLESIAS Pantín, Santiago (1870–1939). Spanish-born working-class organizer and socialist.

MARÍN, Francisco Gonzalo ("Pachín") (1863–1897). Poet, who died fighting for Cuban independence.

MARQUÉS, René (1919–1979). Novelist, short-story writer, essayist and playwright. Perhaps the leading literary figure in Puerto Rico in the 1950s. His most famous play is *La carreta* (1951).

MATIENZO Cintrón, Rosendo (1855–1913). An autonomist before 1898, then a statehooder, later a supporter of independence. Principal organizer of the Independence Party of Puerto Rico (1912).

PALÉS Matos, Luis (1903–1963). Outstanding poet, particularly famous for his Afro-Antillean verses.

RODRÍGUEZ de Tió, Lola (1843–1924). The first Puerto Rican poet to become known in the Caribbean. Lived for many years, and died, in Cuba.

ROMERO Rosa, Ramón (1863–1907). Typographer, worker's organizer and collaborator with Santiago Iglesias. His best-known work is *El emancipación del obrero* (1903).

TAPIA y Riviera, Alejandro (1826–1882). Writer, journalist and outstanding playwright. A book of memoirs, *Mis memorias*, was published posthumously in 1927. For some critics he is the "father of Puerto Rican literature."

VEGA, Bernardo (1885–1965). Tobacco worker, collaborator with Santiago Iglesias, co-founder of the Puerto Rican Socialist Party. Much of his life was spent in New York City.

ZENO Gandía, Manuel (1855–1930). Outstanding novelist. Four of his works, including *La charca* (1894), were grouped together as "Cronícas de un mundo enfermo" (Chronicles of a Sick World).